CLIMBING THE CHARTS

Gabriel Rossman

CLIMBING
THE CHARTS

What Radio Airplay Tells Us
about the Diffusion of Innovation

Princeton University Press   Princeton & Oxford

Copyright © 2012 by Princeton University Press

Published by Princeton University Press,
41 William Street, Princeton, New Jersey 08540
In the United Kingdom: Princeton University Press,
6 Oxford Street, Woodstock, Oxfordshire OX20 1TW

All Rights Reserved

ISBN: 978-0-691-14873-1

Library of Congress Control Number: 2012936278

British Library Cataloging-in-Publication Data is available

This book has been composed in Baskerville 120 Pro and John Sans

Printed on acid-free paper ∞

press.princeton.edu

Typeset by S R Nova Pvt Ltd, Bangalore, India
Printed in the United States of America

10 9 8 7 6 5 4 3 2 1

Paperback ISBN 978-0-691-16671-1

CONTENTS

CONTENTS

FIGURES

ACKNOWLEDGMENTS

This work was supported by several grants. In particular, my first grant was a UCLA faculty senate research grant that allowed early development of the project. The National Science Foundation program in Innovation and Organizational Sciences awarded grant #SES-0724914, "Sustaining and Disruptive Innovation: Drawing Lessons from the Radio Industry." This research made use of facilities and resources at UCLA's California Center for Population Research, which is supported by infrastructure grant R24HD041022 from the Eunice Kennedy Shriver National Institute of Child Health & Human Development. Finally, I received generous support as a Sloan Foundation fellow in industry studies for 2009–2011. These grants facilitated research assistant labor to collect the social network data used in chapter 4, purchases of proprietary monitored airplay and station financial data, and course release time for writing. Of course any opinions, findings, and conclusions, or recommendations expressed in this material are those of the author and do not necessarily reflect the views of the funders.

I presented chapter drafts at various workshops and benefited from feedback there. I presented an early version of chapters 1–3 to both my own colleagues at UCLA sociology and a joint session of Princeton's sociology department and the Center for Arts and Cultural Policy Studies, where Pierre Kremp served as a very useful discussant. I presented chapter 4 both to a mini-conference at UCLA and to the Goizueta Business School at Emory. I presented chapter 5 to the Federal Communications Commission staff economists. Finally, I presented chapter 6 and related research to the Culture and Social Analysis Workshop at Harvard, the Innovation and Creativity Workshop at UCLA's Anderson

School of Management, the American Sociological Association, and my own undergraduates in a freshman seminar "Reggaetón Breaks Into the Mainstream." In addition, Jenn Lena has provided valuable and extensive feedback at all stages of the book, and Cristina Mora provided extensive comments on chapter 6.

Although only chapter 5 overlaps with my dissertation, the work has a strong indirect influence from my advisor, Paul DiMaggio. In the summer of 2000, Paul and I spent many hours discussing diffusion processes and sketching s-curves on the blackboard. I ended up doing my dissertation on a different set of issues and for several years we didn't discuss diffusion, let alone collaborate on it, but in the last few years each of us has returned to focusing on diffusion. How I think as a sociologist in general reflects his supervision of my entire graduate education, and how I think about the specific issues in this book is the result of several conversations about diffusion we had more than ten years ago. Those discussions planted a seed in me that is germinating with this book and related work.

This book benefited greatly from related work with Ming Ming Chiu and Joeri Mol. Together we published an article in *Sociological Methodology* that served as a sort of precursor to the book, especially chapter 3. This article both proposed the idea of interpreting radio programming as a diffusion process and (with the help of Patti Donze) developed a database out of the New York Attorney General's 2004 subpoenaes of music industry records, which I analyzed here in section 3.1.4. Patti also collected the All Music data used in section 6.4.1. In addition Ming, Joeri, and I had many long discussions (which at the time required coordinating schedules across three continents) on the ideas that eventually developed into section 6.3 and figure 3.2.

During the time I worked on this book, I benefited from people in the radio industry. Several programmers (who will remain anonymous) generously consented to qualitative interviews and to pre-test the survey used for chapter 4. Jeff Gelb of Mediabase and Karen Brandt of BIA/fn provided access to airplay and station data. In the media policy community I've had the benefit of talking shop with Peter Alexander, Pete DiCola, Joe Karaganis, Phil Napoli, Paul Porter, George Williams, and especially Kristin Thomson.

UCLA's Academic Technology Services has a world-class set of statistical consultants and I rely on them shamelessly in all of my work, especially Xiao Chen. In addition, UCLA's California Center for Population Research has an excellent set of resources, not the least of which are the center's former and current programmers: David Ash, Laura Piersol, and Aaron Seligman. The readers of my *Code and Culture* blog, especially Kieran Healy, provided useful help with debugging certain problematic bits of code and but for their help I might still be trying to generate the graphs in chapter 4.

UCLA sociology is blessed with many creative and supportive colleagues. I most directly benefited from conversations with and manuscript comments from Bill Roy, Judy Seltzer, Stefan Timmermans, Andreas Wimmer, Lynne Zucker, and several colleagues who provided feedback anonymously as part of my mid-tenure review. Maria Johnson Kriechbaum was an incredibly efficient and conscientious research assistant whose work was invaluable to surveying the radio stations and querying the databases.

While writing this book I spent the better part of two years visiting Harvard. During this time the chairs and staff were very hospitable, granting me access to tangible departmental and campus resources as well as the equally valuable but less tangible benefit of being a welcome guest. The faculty and students at Harvard's sociology department (as well as MIT's Sloan school) are especially good fits for someone interested in culture, economic sociology, and diffusion. I enjoyed the company of many people at Harvard, but this book was most directly influenced by Frank Dobbin, Filiz Garip, Michèle Lamont, Mark Pachucki, and Ezra Zuckerman (MIT).

It has been a delight to work with Eric Schwartz at Princeton University Press. He has consistently been engaged and open and from very early in writing the book I've understood him less as a gatekeeper than a collaborator and supporter. Peer reviewers provided helpful comments and in particular drove me to more explicitly draw out the book's general applications to diffusion of innovation, which were only tacit in the manuscript even though they originally motivated the research.

Nicole Esparza's most direct influence was that chapter 6 was inspired by conversations with her about distinctions between the technical and English definitions of the word "innovation," which led me to understand the importance of seeing trivially new cultural objects being nested within substantively new categories. In addition to serving as muse to this insight, Nicole has been supportive in every aspect of this project, encouraging me to work late and at one point even sending me off for a month to hole up in an undisclosed location. Similarly, my parents not only put me on the path to be where I am but have continued to help during the process of writing this book, most concretely by putting me up when I was commuting between UCLA and Harvard and in helping Nicole, Frances, and I out on a pretty much weekly basis now that we're back.

Finally, I am grateful to live in a society with the intellectual tradition, wealth, and liberty that are the pre-conditions for the exercise of critical inquiry.

CLIMBING THE CHARTS

1

INTRODUCTION

As I wrap up my work on this book, two news items suggest contrary understandings of the role radio plays in American pop culture. The humbling piece of news was that the popular European streaming music service Spotify is entering the American market following successful rights negotiations with the record labels. The service allows instantaneous access to an immense catalog of songs, with the premium version of the service allowing listening on the go over a smart phone or MP3 player. This service joins a variety of other Internet-based music services, including Pandora Radio, Stitcher, Amazon Cloud Player, and Apple's iCloud. These services vary in their details, but all of them provide a more customized listening experience than traditional FM radio.

The other news item was a story from National Public Radio about the pop star Rihanna's single "Man Down."[1] NPR described how Rihanna's label assembled a dream team of songwriters, producers, vocal coaches, and song mixers at a cost of about $78,000 per song. However, this considerable figure was dwarfed by the million dollars it cost to promote a song, about a third of which went to radio promotion. That is, record labels feel it is worth spending in excess of $300,000 to get a song played on the radio. Or perhaps it is better to note that radio airplay is *still* this valuable, despite plummeting recording industry revenues and new media providing alternative avenues to radio's traditional role in making a song a hit.

Taken together, these stories illustrate how FM radio remains an important part of American popular culture even as it competes for listeners with new media. Arbitron's most recent estimates are that the average American over the age of 12 listens to the radio for about 15 hours a week, with the vast majority of this listening being to radio stations that play music.[2] Although this is down considerably from listening rates in the 1990s, 15 hours a week is still a substantial amount of time. Moreover, as seen in the NPR story, this airplay still plays an important role in the broader ecology of pop culture.

The goal of this book is to understand how songs get on the radio. The book examines such issues as corporate radio chains, record label promotion, social networks among stations, and genre conventions. Some of these issues matter less than is commonly believed, others in subtle ways that are not generally understood. Some aspects of these processes are undoubtedly idiosyncratic to the nature of the medium as presently constituted, but others should be general to any process where music spreads through a curated listening experience. Thus, the conclusion of the book will bring us full circle to a consideration of how a better understanding of radio provides a basis for speculating about media that will follow it.

Sociology has approached arts and popular culture as the output of the specific conditions and processes of the culture industries ever since the 1970s.[3] The central insight of this "production of culture" school was to study popular culture not from the perspective of what it means, but how it was made. This emphasis on process reveals the strong influences from and overlaps with economic sociology and organizational sociology. One of the school's main empirical concerns has always been pop music, and in particular the nexus of record labels and radio stations. A central aspect of the process of the music industry is how songs get adopted by radio stations. This is a special case of the general issue of how ideas and practices spread through social fields, which suggests the broader theoretical concerns of the book.

1.1 The Diffusion of Innovation

This book's substantive concern of how songs become hits on the radio is part of a more general class of problems in social science known as the diffusion of innovation. This literature covers a wide variety of substantive areas where actors within a population each decide if and when to adopt an innovation. The seminal studies in this field were about such eclectic phenomena as:

- farmers in Iowa planting a new kind of corn
- firms in heavy industry adopting various new production technologies
- small-town doctors prescribing the antibiotic tetracycline
- postwar households purchasing such appliances as televisions and washing machines[4]

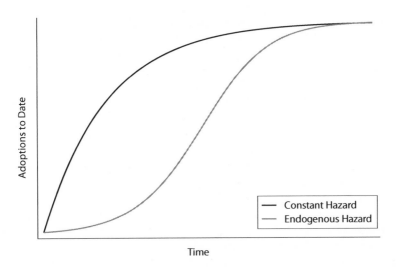

FIGURE 1.1. The Two Ideal Diffusion Curves

The innovations described in the literature range from drastic changes that reorder the actor's cultural and economic experience to fairly minor variations on incumbent practices for which "innovation" is perhaps too grandiose a term. In current sociology, one of the main applications of diffusion analysis is asking such questions as when firms adopt new business practices or how activists adopt new tactics.

At the most basic level, one can study diffusion simply by drawing a graph and looking at its shape to see whether it is more concave or more s-shaped. Figure 1.1 shows typical curves of each ideal type. The shape of the graph is informative because different processes create differently shaped graphs; thus, seeing the shape of the graph gives very strong clues as to the process that created it. In a diffusion graph the x-axis is time, which can be denominated in whatever unit is appropriate. Many of the canonical studies measure time in years, but tetracycline spread in a matter of months, and pop songs usually spread even faster. The y-axis is how popular the innovation is at a particular time. Usually the y-axis is cumulative, showing how many actors have adopted the innovation to date, though sometimes they are plotted as instantaneous, showing how many actors are adopting in each period.

This implies that diffusion is about seeing how many actors adopt the innovation in each period, and it is, but this can be misleading. The reason is that it's quite a different thing for a hundred out of a thousand to adopt than for a hundred out of a hundred. The number of actors who have yet to adopt as of a time is the "risk pool," and the

3

proportion of the risk pool who adopt in a time interval is the "hazard" rate.[5] For a given hazard, the raw number of adoptions decreases as the risk pool shrinks. This is a case of Zeno's paradox, in which fleet-footed Achilles races a tortoise but allows the reptile a head start. If in each minute he closes half the remaining distance, then after the first minute he will have closed 1/2 the distance, after the second minute, 3/4 of the initial gap, then 7/8, 15/16, 31/32, etc. Returning to diffusion, imagine that a thousand doctors have a hazard rate of 10 percent for adopting tetracycline.[6] In the first month 100 doctors (a tenth of 1,000) will write their first prescriptions for tetracycline; in the second month 90 will adopt, for a total of 190 doctors prescribing it; in the third month 81 will adopt, for a total of 271, and so on. In this example the hazard remains constant at one-tenth per month. Therefore, the proportion of the risk pool converted in each period is the same, but the raw volume decreases rapidly. This results in the concave-shaped curve shown in figure 1.1 labeled as "constant hazard," which shows rapid growth initially and asymptotically limited growth thereafter.

So far we have assumed that the hazard is constant. This may be warranted if we imagine that there is some constant force acting in the population and encouraging actors to adopt the innovation, such as a marketing campaign with a fixed budget. For this reason these curves are often known as "external influence" in that the innovation is being spread by something outside of the population adopting it.[7] However, imagine that the innovation is spread as an endogenous process within the population, perhaps by word of mouth. This might be because there is no marketing budget or because the actors simply don't trust advertisements or salesmen to provide impartial advice. For instance, imagine that farmers are deciding to plant a new type of maize that presents higher risk but offers higher reward.[8] Most farmers are hesitant to make so radical a change, but one farmer is willing to experiment with the seed and, on seeing his higher crop yields, he tells two neighbors about his satisfactory experience and they try it. After their own satisfactory experiences they in turn each tell two others. If each person using the corn tells two new neighbors about it, then one farmer will plant it in the first year, three in the second, nine in the fourth, twenty-seven in the fifth, eighty-one in the sixth, and so on. This pattern shows slow diffusion at first, but follows exponential growth so that once the innovation reaches a critical mass of the population, it diffuses rapidly.

Of course there are a finite number of farmers, so the exponential growth cannot continue forever. Once the innovation starts to become popular, many of the people who one might tell about it are in fact already using it, placing exponential growth for the hazard in tension with Zeno's paradox for the risk pool. Contagious diffusion can only occur when someone who has experienced the innovation encounters someone who has not. Diffusion is slow early on because there are too few adopters who can promote the innovation (a low hazard), and it is slow later on because there are so few potential adopters remaining (a small risk pool), but in the middle lies a "tipping point" of intense diffusion where many people are promoting the innovation to many who have yet to adopt it (a high hazard and large risk pool). The resulting graph is the s-shaped curve shown in figure 1.1 and labeled as "endogenous hazard."

Although the example of internal influence described above relies on direct word-of-mouth contagion, the same implications apply to "threshold" or "cascade" models where potential adopters are aware of how many others have adopted the innovation but don't directly communicate with them.[9] For instance, many people who don't make a habit of smashing property and assaulting people on the street will nonetheless join in a sufficiently large riot because safety in numbers means they need be much less afraid of punishment than if they were alone to misbehave. In this model it doesn't matter whether the rioters directly communicate with each other, only that potential rioters have a sense of how large the riot has become. Although in the riot example the potential rioter is directly estimating the size of the mob, this miasmic sort of diffusion is often mediated by things like best-seller lists or website download counts that aggregate and make salient information on popularity.[10] So you may be more likely to buy a book when it becomes a best seller because the book's popularity gives it more conspicuous placement in bookstores, even if you don't personally know a single individual who has read the book or have even observed strangers reading the book in public.

Thus, we have two distinct patterns for how an innovation might diffuse across a population. In the second style, the proportion of holdouts who adopt in each period is determined by how many actors are already using the innovation. Because the hazard rate is a function of prior adoptions, this is an endogenous pattern or an "internal-influence" cycle.[11] In contrast, in the first style a constant proportion of holdouts adopt in every period. Because a constant proportion cannot be a function of how many people have already adopted, it can be interpreted as reflecting an "external-influence" on the system, or an "exogenous" pattern. Of course these patterns are ideal-typical and real cases can approximate one or the other or even a compromise between them. For instance, the diffusion of tetracycline was mostly exogenous, the diffusion of hybrid corn almost perfectly endogenous, and the diffusion of postwar consumer appliances a

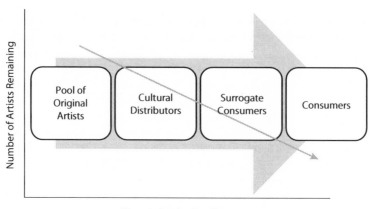

FIGURE 1.2. The Hirsch Gatekeeping Model

compromise between the two patterns.[12] Much of the literature brackets this issue of how different types of innovations spread and instead focus on a single innovation and then ask *which actors* adopted that innovation particularly early. However, in this book I emphasize the question of the nature of diffusion itself and focus on the question of under what circumstances songs follow the concave curve and under which circumstances they follow the s-curve. This is the type of question that cannot be answered by studying a single innovation's diffusion history, but only in comparing those of many innovations, and seeing under what circumstances an innovation's trajectory will follow one path or the other. Such an endeavor requires data on many innovations, and this is a role for which radio singles are well-suited for they occur in such numbers, spread so rapidly, and are so well-documented as to serve the purposes of sociology as admirably as the fruit fly does for those of genetics.

1.2 The Production of Culture

The fundamental model of the popular culture industry used in the production of culture approach was articulated in one of the paradigm's earliest publications, Paul Hirsch's (1972) article in the *American Journal of Sociology*, "Processing Fads and Fashions: An Organization-Set Analysis of Cultural Industry Systems." In figure 1.2, I have distilled Hirsch's model into a schematic. Hirsch saw popular culture as a flow process where cultural objects move downstream from the pool of original artists through cultural distributors and surrogate consumers before reaching the ultimate consumers. Cultural distributors are firms like record labels and book publishers that provide artists with the financing, technical collaborators, retail distribution networks, and other resources to produce their art and get it to market. Surrogate consumers are such actors as radio stations and book reviewers who do not produce art but draw attention to it.

Hirsch gives almost no attention to what goes on within each of these organization-sets, but only in the points of contact between them, an approach consistent with the open systems revolution that was then reshaping organizational theory.[13] So, for example, a record label is most interesting for its A&R (artists and repertoire, i.e., talent scouts)—the point of contact upstream to original artists—and its radio promotion—the point of contact downstream with surrogate consumers.[14] Interestingly, at each of these boundary points there are more failures than successes, which is why the model is described as "gatekeeping." The downward sloping line in figure 1.2 illustrates this progressive winnowing as cultural products move downstream. Only a fraction of original artists find favor with cultural distributors; of those who find favor with distributors, only some are advocated by the surrogate consumers, and of these only some become big hits with consumers. Other early production of culture studies took a similar approach in emphasizing boundary points along the production flow. Most famously Peterson and Berger's (1975) *American Sociological Review* article "Cycles in Symbol Production: The Case of Popular Music" explained the displacement of show tunes by rock and roll in the mid-1950s as being catalyzed by legal and technological shocks that disrupted the ability of cultural distributors (Tin Pan Alley) to co-opt surrogate consumers (radio and film musicals).

Note though that the progressive winnowing through the cultural system is in terms of the diminishing number of artists or titles that find success at each stage. However, through the wonders of electronic reproduction the total volume of fame does not diminish, but grows. That is, at each stage there are fewer successful artists, but those who are successful are so famous that the aggregate of fame increases as one moves downstream. Through the process there are fewer artists attaining more fame, a pattern of massive inequality nicknamed the "superstar effect" which is made possible by the introduction of electronic reproduction.[15] Imagine a set of original artists entering the market, say aspiring musicians. These entrants would be numerous but alike in their obscurity. Only a few of these aspirants would get record contracts, but this alone would give them a modicum of fame. Of those with contracts, only some will gain fame through radio airplay, and of these fewer still will become superstars with the music-consuming public.

7

As successful artists move through the gatekeeping process, their fame develops through a process of accumulation. Some aspects of this can be understood as diffusion of the artist's fame through a population of those at risk of acclaiming the artist. Although at the original artist to cultural distributor boundary there are usually bilateral contracts, surrogate and ultimate consumers are non-exclusive. An artist is only signed to one record company at a time, but a successful pop single will be played by many radio stations and then be purchased by many consumers. Similarly, an academic book only needs one university press (cultural distributor), but aspires to be reviewed in a dozen or so blogs and journal book review sections (surrogate consumers) and read by thousands of colleagues and students (consumers). That is, while the original artist to distributor boundary is a one-to-one issue of two actors signing a contract, the distributor-surrogate and surrogate-consumer boundaries are one-to-many issues of many actors each adopting a product. This of course is a diffusion process and can be modeled as such. Like much of the seminal production of culture literature discussed above, this book focuses especially on the boundary between cultural distributors and surrogate consumers and the nature of the relationship between them. Treating this issue as a diffusion process allows us to see how surrogate consumers collectively decide to pass a cultural object through their stage in the gatekeeping process. As discussed throughout this book, the surrogate consumers' criteria that underly this decision may include the influence of the upstream distributors, various peer dynamics among the surrogate consumers, political pressure, or genre conventions.

1.3 Organization of the Book

Throughout this book I discuss different aspects of radio airplay of pop music from the perspective of diffusion analysis. The central problem throughout these chapters is how songs become hits, and each chapter emphasizes a different aspect of this issue.

Chapter 2 shows that the number of stations that have played a pop song follows a pattern consistent with all of the radio stations reacting to something outside of their peer group. This implies a puzzle that if radio stations are not imitating one another, from whom exactly are they taking their cues? The rest of the chapter demonstrates that the stations are not reacting to the mere availability of a song when a record drops, nor are the much maligned radio chains coordinating the add dates of their properties.

Chapter 3 argues that this centralizing coordination comes from the promotional efforts of record labels, as seen in extreme form with payola. The chapter reviews all four payola scandals since 1960. Over the last 50 years, payola has involved greatly varying degrees of subtlety and tact but always involved various forms of cash or in-kind compensation being exchanged for airplay. Ironically, the most "professional" forms of payola are those where the exchange is elaborately obfuscated by being embedded in in-kind gift exchange. A time series of the estimated influence of record label influence over airplay during the most recent scandal and qualitative review of older scandals show how rapidly the payola exchange network reconstitutes itself after a disruption, and the chapter closes with a theoretical argument as to why payola is so robust.

Chapter 4 applies the "opinion leaders" hypothesis to radio—a field that has its own folk version of the theory. Opinion leadership is a special case of contagious diffusion in which actors at the center of a social network exert a special power to influence diffusion through the network. To test this idea I collected social network data in a survey of Top 40 stations. Consistent with the theory, I find that there are some particularly esteemed stations, but contrary to the theory there is nothing special about when they begin playing a song. The remainder of the chapter argues that peer group dynamics are a scope condition for opinion leadership, but even when this condition is met, we still fail to see a special opinion leadership role for the core stations.

Chapter 5 presents a case history of the Dixie Chicks radio boycott. Shortly before the start of the Iraq war, the Dixie Chicks were at the top of the charts in Country and Adult Contemporary. Then, after their lead singer insulted President George W. Bush, the band lost almost all of its airplay. Commentators at the time blamed large radio chains, but I show that the big chains were, if anything, slower to blacklist the musicians than were small radio companies. Rather, I find that the speed with which stations blacklisted the band was mostly a function of the political climate of the station's locales and of country music as a genre.

Chapter 6 discusses the implications of the long-term trend for radio to be segmented into ever narrower formats as a special case of the general issue of art classification systems. A discussion of crossover between formats shows how diffusion patterns are qualitatively different for a song's home format than for those formats to which it crosses over, with stations being much more hesitant and attentive to peer behavior when the genre fit is dubious. This of course raises the question of how genres emerge in the first place, an issue explored with a case study of the popularity of reggaetón and the associated rise of the "Hurban" radio format.

Finally, the conclusion to the book discusses the long-term relative decline and recent absolute decline of radio as a medium and the rise of the media that are replacing it. In order to extrapolate lessons to these emerging media, the conclusion reviews the findings of the rest of the book. By taking these findings and applying them to an emerging landscape, we cannot only understand the findings themselves better but also what the production of culture will look like once radio has been eclipsed.

A Note on Style

This book discusses both music genres and radio formats. Although in some cases (e.g., country) genre and format are nearly coterminous, in most cases a format is a blend of genres. As a stylistic convention borrowed from some of the radio literature, throughout the book I use lowercase whenever referring to music genres and uppercase whenever referring to radio formats. For instance, "Rhythmic stations mostly play hip-hop music" or "country music is played almost exclusively on Country stations."

2

HOW SONGS SPREAD

The central empirical concern of this book is how songs become popular on the radio, so a good place to start is by case study of a particularly successful song. In figure 2.1, I have graphed the diffusion curve for "Umbrella" by Rihanna. Although the song was also popular in several other formats, I limit this to "Top 40" stations (all of which played "Umbrella" sooner or later) to avoid any confounding effects of format.[1] This 2007 duet with Jay-Z was Rihanna's seventh hit song since her 2005 debut. The song spread explosively and then slowed thereafter. As many stations started playing the song in its first three weeks as did so over the next year.[2] Indeed, 22 percent of Top 40 stations began playing the song on its first *day*. As discussed in the previous chapter, this concave growth pattern is consistent with an exogenous process and is entirely inconsistent with the s-shaped curves produced by an endogenous process. It is completely implausible to argue that radio stations decided to play this song because they were imitating each other, as its popularity simply happened too fast for stations to be attentive to each other. This is true whether one expects that stations might imitate specific peer stations (a contagious diffusion dynamic) or that they might imitate the radio industry as a whole as summarized by the pop charts (a threshold diffusion dynamic), a distinction that will be explored more fully in chapter 4. Either way we would expect to see an s-curve, but we do not.

That we do not see an s-curve but rather a concave curve implies that this song did *not* spread across radio as an endogenous process of the kind so beloved by sociologists, popular science writers, and "viral marketing" consultants. As will be explored in later chapters, under some circumstances songs do demonstrate endogenous

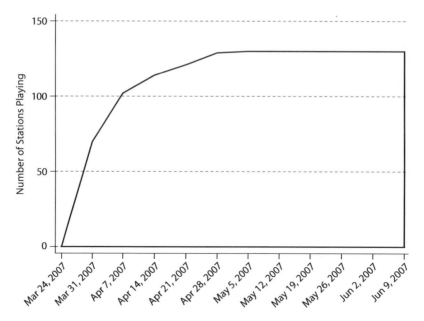

FIGURE 2.1. Diffusion Curve for "Umbrella" by Rihanna on Top 40 Stations

processes. Nonetheless, in general, pop songs have concave curves with the same shape that we see for "Umbrella," though of course most songs do not get as big.[3] To explain how so many radio stations came to play "Umbrella," we cannot resort to arguments about contagion or cascades. Rather, we must look to something apart from peer influence to explain why so many radio stations started playing the song so quickly, without waiting to see if their peers would play it first. This something may be a trait of the song itself or it may be some actor who is influencing all of the radio stations.

The rest of this chapter will explore two plausible explanations for why stations seem to add songs in response to something outside the population of stations. The first is that stations have unsated demand for new music from pop stars and play songs as soon as they are available. The second is that the large companies who have dominated radio since deregulation coordinate the airplay of their properties. In both cases I will show the implications of these putative causes and test whether they are consistent with the evidence.

2.1 Record Release Dates

One of the most obvious reasons to expect such rapid diffusion is unsated demand. We might imagine that when a beloved artist releases

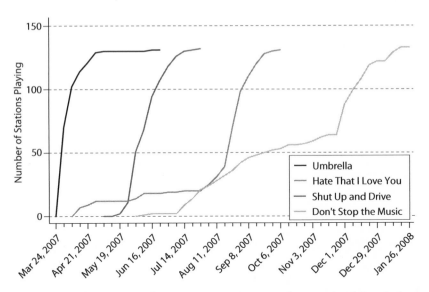

FIGURE 2.2. Diffusion Curves for Singles on the Rihanna Album *Good Girl Gone Bad* on Top 40 Stations

new music, radio stations would immediately jump at the chance to play it. If we make certain realistic assumptions about the distribution of unsated demand for an artist across radio stations, we might imagine that unsated demand would produce the observed pattern of rapid diffusion followed by slow diffusion. There are two problems with this interpretation. First, unsated demand sounds plausible for explaining the diffusion of songs by established stars, but we would not imagine that radio stations were eagerly awaiting releases by hitherto unknown performers. We might imagine that when songs by unknown artists do spread, they would tend to do so through endogenous patterns, with a few stations taking a chance and this behavior influencing rivals. In fact, contrary to the predictions of the unsated demand hypothesis, songs by unknown artists tend to diffuse by an exogenous pattern, though not as steeply or as widely as those by stars.[4] A more severe problem for the unsated demand explanation is that it cannot explain why multiple songs from the same album become popular at different times.

As seen in figure 2.2, "Umbrella" was only the first hit song from Rihanna's double platinum album *Good Girl Gone Bad*, which also included "Shut Up and Drive," "Hate That I Love You," and "Don't Stop the Music."[5] It is understandable that "Umbrella" spread earlier as it was released before the rest of the album. However, when *Good Girl Gone Bad* was released in record stores on June 5, 2007, radio

13

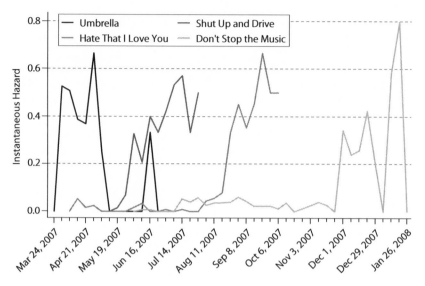

FIGURE 2.3. Hazards for Singles on the Rihanna Album *Good Girl Gone Bad* on Top 40 Stations

stations had available to them 11 more songs, all of which critics thought had the potential to be hits and three of which ultimately achieved this status. Despite this abundance of new material available from a hot young star, radio stations showed remarkable conformity in choosing which songs to add to playlists first. With few exceptions, radio stations began playing "Umbrella" in March, "Shut Up and Drive" in June, "Hate That I Love You" in late summer, and "Don't Stop the Music" within a few weeks of Christmas. In each case the pattern is basically consistent with an exogenous diffusion process beginning at the respective dates.

For each of these three Rihanna songs that became popular after "Umbrella," there is some growth leading up to the wave, but the wave itself occured suddenly.[6] This can be seen more clearly by looking at figure 2.3, which shows the hazard rates (rather than the cumulative number of stations playing the songs as in figure 2.2). For instance, between May and Thanksgiving, "Don't Stop the Music" inched its way across radio with an average hazard rate of less than 1 percent of holdout stations adopting per week. However at this point the diffusion process appears to change, with the song spreading much more rapidly, and thereafter the hazard is about 3 percent of holdout stations adopting per week. The change in the hazard before and after Thanksgiving is too abrupt to be consistent with an endogenous tipping point (which should show a hazard that increases exponentially, but not as a step function). Rather, what we see is that overnight the hazard jumps and the curve becomes consistent with a strong exogenous force taking effect on that date. At any given time, exactly one song from the *Good Girl Gone Bad* album has a high hazard rate. This lasts about two months and then moves on to the next song. If the reason that radio stations tend to start playing a song all at once was that they all gained access to it at the same time, this supposition fails to explain why most radio stations sat on "Hate That I Love You" and "Don't Stop the Music" for weeks or months after the songs became available and then suddenly began playing them during a very short time window. As seen in appendix B, this pattern is even more clear if we define "begin playing" more stringently, in which case the early adoptions of each song disappear. Since the simple fact of songs being made available to radio stations is not enough to explain the tremendous conformity of radio stations, we must look for an actor who coordinates radio. Who is it who decides which song is going to spread?

2.2 Corporate Radio

Anyone familiar with debates over the state of radio will immediately recognize that many people have a strong idea as to exactly who is the central actor who coordinates radio: Clear Channel Communications.[7] The San Antonio-based company owns about one in ten of all commercial American radio stations and is widely believed to centralize programming decisions.

The back story for Clear Channel's role in the radio industry is the Telecommunications Act of 1996, the first major overhaul of telecom law since 1934. Most of the Telecom Act is about promoting competition between cable and phone companies in the markets for voice communications, television entertainment, and broadband Internet service. In a provision that was little noted at the time, the act also eliminated the cap of 20 AM and 20 FM stations at the national level and considerably relaxed ownership caps at the local level. During the four years following deregulation, radio went from an industry where no company owned more than 40 stations to a situation where Clear Channel owned more than 1,000 stations and several rivals owned more than 100 stations each.[8] The top ten companies together owned 290 stations in 1995 versus 2,504 in 2005. The changes are even more skewed for revenues, with the Herfindahl-Hirschman Index of industrial concentration climbing from 81 in 1993 to 1,046 in 2004.[9]

One of the implications of conglomeration is that companies can achieve economies of scale by centralizing programming. As a Future of Music Coalition (FMC) report rhetorically asks, "[r]adio parent companies are eager to take advantage of economies of scale to cut costs, after all, why have three programming directors for three Top 40 stations, when there are cost savings in having just one?"[10] Indeed, radio stations are now understaffed by historical standards. This leaner staffing, coupled with industry conglomeration and new technology, presents implications for programming practices:

> New technologies and organizational strategies have indeed arisen in the wake of the Telecommunications Act. First, large radio companies can now adopt "voice tracking" technology. Voice tracking is the practice of broadcasting the show of a famous radio announcer (or DJ) nationwide while trying to make the show seem local. Radio companies can enjoy the cost savings that accompany syndication while appearing to tailor its programming to communities' needs. Second, radio companies now plan much of their programming centrally. DJs have less choice; market-testing of ten-second song snippets has become prevalent; and payola-like practices have allegedly affected programming decisions. To the extent that more programming decisions occur centrally, fewer DJs and program directors are needed.[11]

Both of these changes imply that programming will be accomplished more centrally; the only difference is whether on-air talent is also centralized. To the extent such practices are implemented, programming will no longer be a local issue.

These allegations of centralized programming have testable implications that should be observable in the diffusion curves. Let us then think through the implications of a diffusion process based on centralized chain decision-making by starting with the extreme case and gradually imagining more subtle scenarios. To start, imagine that Clear Channel did not have any local programmers at all. Rather, in this counterfactual, a programmer at corporate headquarters in San Antonio creates a single playlist for all of the company's stations.[12] This playlist would then either be e-mailed to local disk jockeys or, better yet, there would be no local disk jockeys and the broadcasts would be piped in from a central recording studio 24 hours a day via syndication or voice tracking. In this scenario, all Clear Channel stations would have identical content and therefore would show the same adoption behavior, adding any given song on exactly the same day.[13] If we imagine the diffusion curve just for Clear Channel stations, in this scenario it would not be a curve at all but a step function, with the level of adoption going from zero stations to all stations overnight.

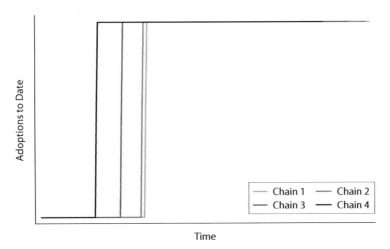

FIGURE 2.4. Illustration of the Corporate "Single Playlist" Hypothesis

Another testable implication can be derived from noting that nobody alleges that Clear Channel controls *all* of radio, only the sizable proportion of stations that it owns. Therefore, even if Clear Channel coordinates the behavior of its own stations, we would not expect it to also coordinate the behavior of stations owned by its rivals. Even if other stations (or station chains) imitated Clear Channel's behavior there would nonetheless be a lag, as they would only observe Clear Channel's behavior, not its planned behaviors. Likewise, if other major chains like Cumulus and CBS had centralized programming, this would only directly affect the stations in their chains and their step functions would be randomly offset from that of Clear Channel. Thus, a strong degree of coordination implies a vertical curve for each chain; however, these vertical curves would vary randomly from chain to chain. I have illustrated this hypothesis in figure 2.4. Statistically inclined readers can interpret the "single playlist" hypothesis as the expectation that most of the variance in add dates is *between* chains, but there is little or no variance *within* chains.

To test this hypothesis, I plotted "Umbrella" again in figure 2.5, but this time with a separate curve for each company with an appreciable number of Top 40 stations. As can be seen, the companies each show the same smooth exogenous diffusion curve. This result contrasts strikingly with what we would expect were decisions made at the chain level. First, note that no chain shows a step function with all of its stations adopting in the same week. Rather, each chain shows a smooth diffusion curve among its stations. Second, the curves are essentially identical with

17

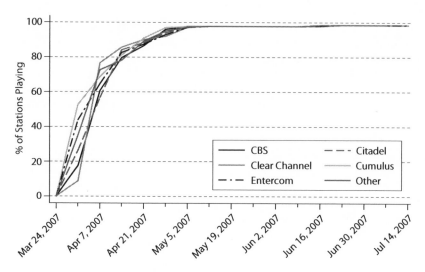

FIGURE 2.5. Diffusion Curves for "Umbrella" by Rihanna for Top 40 Stations Owned by Various Chains

only trivial and probably random discrepancies between the adoption times of stations in different chains. If a single playlist were circulated among Clear Channel stations and a different single playlist among CBS stations, we would expect both companies to show step functions and for a gap to exist between them. That this is not the case implies that we can rule out the possibility of strong coordination at the chain level to explain the rapid popularity of "Umbrella."

Of course, it's one thing to show that a particular song is not appreciably clustered by corporate owner. It is a much stronger claim to show that overall song diffusion is *not at all* explained by corporate ownership. For one thing, it may be that "Umbrella" is just a fluke—perhaps in March 2007 the fax machine at Clear Channel's corporate headquarters was broken. For another, perhaps there is chain influence but it is subtle enough so as to not be apparent by eyeballing one song at a time, but still substantial in the aggregate. A single playlist used by all the stations in a chain (within a format) would be immediately visible in the diffusion curves, but it is possible to imagine coordination at the chain level more subtle than this, yet still with important effects. That is, there are many ways that we might imagine a situation where a large radio chain would promulgate information useful for programming internally. For instance, a radio chain might have a chief programmer at the corporate level who creates projections, conducts audience surveys, analyzes sales data, and simply provides informed aesthetic judgments and then shares all of this valuable insight with programmers working at the various stations in his or her chain. This information would not be used automatically but interpreted and applied slightly differently by each station in the company. In other words, we might imagine that corporate would not send out orders, but provide advice. In this scenario we would expect each chain to exhibit a smooth exogenous function (rather than a step function). However, because each company would provide different information to its stations at a different time than would rival chains, we would still expect each of these chain-specific curves to be offset from each other. Another mechanism with similar effects might be intracompany social networks.[14] Some evidence suggests that practices do especially spread between radio stations in the same company.[15] Likewise in my survey of social networks among Top 40 stations (described in more detail in chapter 4), several programmers reported regular conference calls between corporate sister stations in which they shared information and ideas on programming decisions. Such a tendency for stations to especially form intracorporate social networks might lead to clustering of their programming.

Thus, we can imagine several ways for there to be considerable coordination by chain that would be less blatant than that implied by the extreme "single playlist" hypothesis and might be hard to see just by looking at one song. We might attempt to answer this question by drawing curves for hundreds of songs; however, the question is better answered by regression analysis. Not only is this more concise and allows for more formal testing, but it also allows us to keep information about clustering within small chains rather than just lumping them in the "other" category. To test this I collected a sample of songs. Because event history analysis can only interpret reasonably popular innovations, I limited the sample to songs that were played on the radio at least 5,000 times. I then collected a stratified random sample of 100 of these popular songs per year for 2002–2007.

For each of these songs, I found in which format the song was most popular, and among the stations in that format, I analyzed whether corporate sister stations had especially similar add dates. To do this I used survival time regression models with shared frailty by ownership and no fixed parameters. Shared frailty is the special tendency of two actors (such as radio stations) within an identifiable cluster (such as a corporation) to do the same thing (such as play a particular song) at the same time.[16] I have one analysis for each of the sampled songs, and each of these analyses produces an estimate of how much the otherwise unexplained variance in station add dates for that song is clustered by the stations' corporate owners. Although this is a somewhat

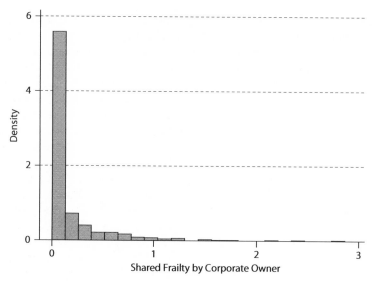

FIGURE 2.6. Distribution of Song Adoption Time Clustering by Corporate Owner

complex concept, for our purposes the interpretation is simply that a high degree of shared frailty implies that stations within the same corporation are especially likely to start playing the song at the same or similar times. Because we get this estimate for each song, the big picture for radio overall is best conceived of as a distribution of the frailty estimates, shown in figure 2.6 as a histogram.

What this plot shows us is that, for the vast majority of songs, there is essentially no shared frailty by corporate chain, but for a tiny fraction of songs there is rather a lot. Of course this is difficult to interpret because we would expect even random noise to show some association, but how much?[17] To test this I contrasted the analyses of observed data with analyses of random data. To do this I repeated the analysis for each song a hundred times, but in these repetitions I shuffled the station's add time and its owner. That is, I kept the actual distribution of chain ownership and the actual diffusion curve, but I broke any association between them. Any perceived shared frailty with these analyses of random data is a pure coincidence and thus we have a good baseline for what purely random clustering by corporate owner should look like.[18] In fact, the estimate for the average amount of shared frailty based on the observed data is entirely typical of the estimates of average shared frailty based on the runs using randomized data.[19] In other words, the extent to which sister stations especially cluster their add times is no greater than what we would expect by chance.

In this chapter, we have seen that pop songs usually spread among radio stations in a way that is inconsistent with the stations imitating one another but is consistent with some central force influencing all of the stations. Because the same pattern applies to later singles on an album, the pattern cannot be explained by album release dates. Likewise, popular speculation attributes conformity among radio stations to corporate ownership, but we have strong evidence that corporate radio chains do *not* centrally coordinate the decision to add songs to radio playlists.[20] This is not to say that there is no force at all organizing the adoption behavior of radio stations. Indeed, given the constant hazard function revealed by song diffusion curves, it is clear that they are all reacting independently to some central coordinating force and they are definitely not just imitating each other. Thus there is central coordination in radio, but it is not coming from Clear Channel or CBS headquarters, which leaves open the question of what *is* causing radio stations to so tightly coordinate their behavior? A more promising suspect will be identified in the next chapter.

3

BUYING YOUR WAY ONTO
THE CHART

In the last chapter I established that something is making radio stations behave as though they were coordinated by a central actor, but that surprisingly this coordination does not come from the corporate radio chains. Still, this leaves open the question of exactly who *is* coordinating radio. One way to begin to answer the question is to think of the long-running (but now defunct) trade journal *Radio and Records* and see the radio industry as part of a broader music industry that includes such actors as instrument manufacturers, live performance promoters and venues, and most important of all, the recorded music industry. The recorded music industry is roughly the same size as the radio broadcasting industry and the two are tightly inter-connected, with the radio industry relying on recorded music for content and the recorded music industry relying on radio for promotion.

Consider that it is rare for a person to walk into WalMart or Best Buy or to log onto Amazon or iTunes and purchase music that they have never heard before. Most of the time we either have a specific purchase in mind or we browse until we recognize something that prior familiarity has taught us is worth $1.29 for an iTunes single or $14.99 for a compact disc. While we sometimes buy music based purely on a friend recommending it to us or after having heard it performed live, most of the time we buy music based on having been exposed to it through broadcast media, especially pop music radio. Even if we are already longtime fans of a band, broadcasting usually motivates the decision by making us aware of the new album and by convincing us that the new album is as good as the previous ones, not to mention that when we first developed a taste for the band a few years ago it was probably through broadcasting. In short, airplay is a major determinant of sales. The core theme of Jacob Slichter's candid memoir of one-hit-wonderdom can be summed up as "There is no better guarantor of a band's success than a hit single on the radio luring listeners into record stores to buy the album."[1] Similarly, the gatekeeping model discussed in chapter 1 emphasizes how such "surrogate consumers" as radio effectively mediate between cultural distributors (e.g., record labels) and the ultimate consumers.

In part this is simply because broadcasting is an efficient way for us to become aware of music. However, there is also a certifying function above and beyond the simple fact of awareness. Our taste in cultural products is profoundly, even dominantly, shaped by perceptions of popularity, which we interpret as a signal of quality.[2] When radio stations play music, they are not just making us aware of songs, but suggesting that they are already popular. It is in this respect that the supposed impartiality of gatekeepers like radio stations makes their endorsements more valuable than advertising.

If airplay drives sales, then this implies that airplay is a nearly essential resource for pop musicians and their record labels. Record labels therefore go to great lengths to get airplay. The most basic practice is that record labels deluge radio programmers and other workers in the music industry with promotional copies of CDs in the hopes that they will be impressed by the music and give it airplay and other exposure.[3] In addition, record labels employ large staffs of workers tasked with promoting music to radio stations. Often these promotional workers are responsible for a specific territory and hence are known as "locals." In essence, then, a big part of the label strategy for getting airplay is to expose radio workers to their music and give them a series of sales pitches touting the music's virtues.

Ultimately though, the most direct way to get airplay is to bribe a radio station (or its employees) to play your music. Indeed, this is often exactly what happens, and the amounts involved can be substantial. Record label executives and a leading payola broker estimated the total volume of the market in the early 1980s as between $50 million and $80 million a year.[4] Likewise, in an October 2001 e-mail, an Entercom executive estimated how much each of his stations was worth to record labels or their proxies and gave the expectation that each of his stations raise that much value, with estimates at about $75,000–$125,000 for stations in such youth-oriented formats as Alternative and Top 40 and less for stations in older-skewing formats like Adult Contemporary. Extrapolating the Entercom figures to the industry as a whole and adjusting for inflation gives a ballpark estimate comparable to that in the 1980s.

Payola is a broad family of practices with a wide gray zone that shades into legitimate promotion techniques. The most direct form of payola is simply a *quid pro quo* where a station (or the station's staff) agrees to play a particular song in exchange for cash, intellectual property rights, drugs, or sex. Most often payola is channeled through independent radio promoters and in-kind gifts. Independent radio promoters (IRPs or indies) are consultants who help record labels get airplay.[5] Some of the services provided by indies are legitimate consulting, such as helping a label professionally package a CD and promotional mailer or crafting a sales pitch appropriate to a particular format. Such legitimate services are particularly important for small record labels that are too small to maintain a full in-house promotional staff, but this kind of outsourcing could be valuable even to a large record label since the indie may be expert on a locale or music genre that was previously unfamiliar to the label. However, indies are also known to commonly engage in money laundering. One way this works is that an indie keeps a station on retainer by buying its playlist.[6] Since the monitored airplay databases update the playlists for most commercial stations every night, there is no real reason for the indies to buy playlists directly from the station. Rather, buying a playlist is a legal fiction that allows the indie a pretext for paying the station for access to and influence with the program director and music director. The involvement of indies keeps both the record label and the radio station ignorant of exactly how the payola process works, which serves them by creating plausible deniability but also allows indies to extract brokerage rents.

In the remainder of this chapter I will first review each of the four broadcasting-era payola scandals. This history shows both how payola has changed over time and how the underlying nature of the transaction remains similar, even after the practice was purged of its most unsavory elements in 1986. I will then present a time-series analysis of the most recent payola scandal, showing how transitory an effect it had on the ability of record labels to influence radio. Finally, I use game theory to explain why the natural equilibrium of the music industry is to be characterized by payola, even though the recording industry would prefer to be free of the expense.

3.1   A History of Payola Scandals

Despite furtive and obfuscatory exchange, payola occasionally becomes notorious. Figure 3.1 illustrates the number of stories including the words "payola" and "radio" in the *New York Times*. As can be seen there was a huge wave of stories in 1959, when the term first reached the general public, and never again reaches such prominence. However,

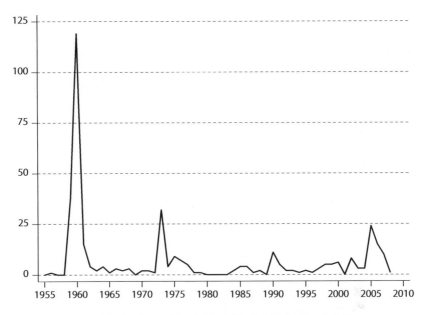

FIGURE 3.1. Stories on "Payola" and "Radio" in the *New York Times*

a series of much smaller jumps occurred in 1973, 1990, and 2005, implying that there is a payola scandal about every 15 years. Furthermore, if one reads the actual stories it becomes apparent that almost all of the stories in the off years are referring to the four main scandals and not reporting newly suspected instances of payola. Since all four of these payola scandals are well-documented, it is worth examining them in detail to understand how payola works, what implications it has for airplay, and why the scandals occur at such a regular interval.

3.1.1   The 1950s Scandal and the Rise of Rock and Roll

The original payola scandal came in the late 1950s as part of the long-standing rivalry between two royalty agencies: American Society of Composers, Authors, and Publishers (ASCAP, supported by Tin Pan Alley and holding mostly show tunes and classical music) and Broadcast Music, Inc. (BMI, supported by broadcasters and holding mostly country, rock, and R&B).[7] ASCAP had been losing market share to BMI and it blamed this decline on a variety of cozy relationships that BMI had with broadcasters, including allegations of payola. At ASCAP's instigation, Senator George Smathers (D-FL) introduced a bill into Congress in 1958 to bar cross-ownership of record companies and

25

broadcasting by the same company under the logic that such cross-owned broadcasters might favor records released by their sister record labels.[8] The hearings included accusations that both payola and cross-ownership were responsible for the rapid displacement of traditional Tin Pan Alley pop music by rock and roll and other genre music in 1956. While later analyses have shown that payola was only partially responsible for the creative destruction of 1950s pop music, such a nefarious explanation pandered to the conservative tastes of the Senate, among whose ranks there were no teeny boppers.[9] Throughout the various payola hearings in 1958 and 1959, congressmen and regulators were persistently bewildered that any disk jockey in his right mind would prefer rock and roll over show tunes absent inducement, a suspicion that was corroborated by cooperating witnesses flipped by the committee.

In 1959, the House of Representatives Committee on Legislative Oversight (or the Kefauver Committee) investigated the quiz show scandal, most remembered for Professor Charles van Doren's confession that the producers of *21* helped him cheat. In late 1959, the committee uncovered evidence of what are known today as "product shots."[10] The Tin Pan Alley camp took the opportunity to tip-off the committee about pop music payola. The Tin Pan Alley composer and American Guild of Authors and Composers president Burton Lane submitted a letter amply documented with articles from trade magazines that explained how product shots worked with pop music. Furthermore, this tip-off came a few months after the broadcasting industry did its reputation no favors by hosting the notorious Second Annual Radio Programming Seminar and Pop Music Disk Jockey Festival in Miami, a week-long event at which the record labels plied thousands of disk jockeys with prostitutes and prodigious quantities of alcohol.[11]

In response to Lane's letter, the House convened the Harris hearings on "payola and other deceptive practices." Two themes that emerged were that payola was pervasive and that it was key to the rise of rock and roll. Witnesses testified that bribes were often naked payments but also took the form of paying disk jockeys for side work, such as consulting or personal appearances at dances, as well as giving disk jockeys equity stakes in pop songs.[12] Of particular interest was Dick Clark, whose popular program *Bandstand* had a suspicious tendency to book artists in whom his publishing and record companies had a stake. Clark denied culpability but ended the conflict of interest by divesting these companies. The Federal Trade Commission held its own hearings and discovered that such equity stakes by disk jockeys were common and often took the form of a share of royalties. The most notable case of this is "Maybellene," one of the first rock and roll songs whose publishing rights are split between Chuck Berry, who actually wrote and performed the song, and Alan Freed, who popularized the song by putting it in heavy rotation on his radio program. The conclusion to the original payola scandal was that in 1960, Congress made it a federal offense to give personal bribes to broadcaster employees. Bribing the broadcasting firm was already illegal, but until the 1990s payola was mostly personal bribes given to disk jockeys and programmers rather than to stations. In practical terms the law shifted primary responsibility for prosecuting payola from the FTC to the Federal Communications Commission and the Department of Justice.

3.1.2   The 1973 Drugola Scandal

The next major payola scandal came in 1973 as the by-product of a drug bust. In February of that year, a joint investigation by the federal government and the Royal Canadian Mounted Police resulted in the indictment of the New Jersey talent agent and gangster Pasquale Falcone for such crimes as importing 20 pounds of heroin through Montreal. Searches of his papers revealed that Falcone had also used a fictitious trucking company to bill false invoices to Columbia Records with the cooperation of David Wynshaw, the head A&R man at Columbia. The government searched Wynshaw's office and found documents showing that Wynshaw had helped his boss, Clive Davis, misappropriate funds from the company for such purposes as remodeling Davis's apartment.[13] At this time Davis had worked at Columbia Records for seven years, the last two of them as president, and was generally credited with the company's belated but fantastically successful transition from Tin Pan Alley to rock music. Columbia hired a law firm to perform an ethics audit and fired Wynshaw and Davis, suing the latter to recover the embezzled funds. Although Davis was convicted of tax evasion, he went on to refute Fitzgerald's aphorism about "no second acts in American lives" by almost immediately landing a job at Arista Records. Decades later, Davis is still a powerful figure in the music industry.

After being presented with evidence against him, Wynshaw decided to cooperate with the government and testified extensively about both the mafia and Columbia's payola practices. In 1972, soul music was taking an increasing share of the pop charts and—as record companies often do when a new genre emerges—Columbia responded to this by either acquiring outright or signing distribution deals with several small labels specializing in the new genre.[14] Wynshaw testified that shortly thereafter Columbia began supporting this product line with payola amounting to at least $250,000 a year. Among the recipients of these bribes was the publisher of a music tip sheet who kept some of the money for skewing his publication and passed along the rest as bribes to radio station personnel. In other cases record producers and indies handled it. Most of the bribes apparently went to disk jockeys, despite changes to the radio industry in the 1960s to reduce their autonomy.[15] A novel twist was that much of the payola was in the form of cocaine and heroin rather than cash and thus this episode is sometimes referred to as the "drugola" scandal. Conservative writers and politicians such as William Safire and Senator James Buckley (Conservative–NY) saw this incident, along with the recent overdoses of Janis Joplin and Jimi Hendrix, as indicative of the degree to which drugs had saturated rock music and called for further journalistic and governmental investigations to this effect.[16]

3.1.3 The Gambino Family and "The Network" in the 1980s

The outcry over drugola and the CBS ethics audit were apparently ineffective. In 1986, NBC News reported on the existence of "the Network," a cartel of about a dozen independent radio promoters tied to the Gambino mafia family.[17] The story included testimony from a disk jockey that indies affiliated with the Network had offered him cash and cocaine and from a competing independent radio promoter who claimed the Network had threatened him with violence. It closed with footage of a meeting between several members of the Network and the gangster John Gotti. Three days later, U.S. Attorney Rudy Giuliani issued subpoenas to the Recording Industry Association of America and the record labels. In response, the record labels issued a statement announcing they would no longer deal with indies. While Warner and CBS had made a brief unsuccessful attempt to boycott the indies in 1981, the 1986 boycott was more successful because all of the major labels joined and all of them feared further legal exposure to the U.S. Attorney's investigation.

At this point Giuliani lost interest in the case and it was turned over to his colleagues in Los Angeles, who focused on the indie Joe Isgro and his partner Ralph Tashjian. Isgro had long been a target of the Los Angeles Police Department's organized crime unit because he seemed to have close ties to the Gambino family, especially the underboss Joseph "Piney" Armone. In 1988, Isgro's former bodyguard, David Michael Smith, returned from England (where he had been avoiding a subpoena from Giuliani) and agreed to cooperate with prosecutors. In 1990, a federal grand jury indicted Isgro for racketeering, mail fraud, and distributing cocaine. Several days into the trial, the judge suspended the case—and ultimately dismissed it with prejudice—because the prosecution failed to divulge to the grand jury or the defense that a key prosecution witness was contradicting his own testimony from an earlier trial, which implies perjury suborned by the prosecutor.[18] Nonetheless the Isgro (mis)trial was well-publicized and received far more press coverage than the events in 1986 that presaged it.

Whatever the procedural and ethical errors in the prosecution, the trial provided a revealing portrait of payola in the 1980s.[19] During this period, record labels spent at least $50 million a year on the Network, with Isgro alone taking receipts of about $10 million a year. The system worked such that members of the Network claimed particular radio stations as their territory. When a station started playing a song, the indie who claimed the station would bill the record label for the add.[20] If labels refused to pay, they would find their artists blacklisted from the station until the indie was appeased. In exchange for allowing indies control over their airplay, radio station personnel would receive cash payments, often stuffed into record sleeves. In the Isgro case, Smith testified that he routinely handled briefcases with $100,000 in cash which was parceled out in units of several thousand dollars to programmers, other indies, and Piney Armone. Likewise, a disk jockey testified that Tashjian would often send him an eighth of cocaine hidden inside of an audio cassette. In a separate prosecution, a Network subcontractor, Howard Goodman, was convicted of bribing radio programmers by sending them birthday cards stuffed with tens of thousands of dollars in cash.[21] Altogether, the indies so effectively controlled radio during this period that they could exclude songs for which bribes were not paid. Thus, it is perhaps more appropriate to think of payola in the early 1980s as being more of stations and indies *extorting* the labels than the labels and indies *bribing* the stations.

Although the prosecutors botched the 1990 Isgro trial, the 1986 major label boycott of indies *was* effective at restructuring the relationship between labels, indies, and stations. First, while the labels did not indefinitely preserve their commitment to avoid dealing with indies, they reallocated the expense from a general budget item to artist support. The consequence is that since 1986, indie billings have been recoupable debt against royalties and this has made artists share the expense with the labels.[22] Joe Isgro described the change as follows:

> What the labels wanted to do was move the cost of indie promotion to the artist. That's what they're doing. The companies funnel money through management and tour support, and it gets paid to us with their full knowledge and direction. They have deferred that cost, charging it back to artist royalties. I think it was a brilliant move.[23]

The other major change was that the independent radio promoters reformed their business practices. The Network cartel, with its mob connections, envelopes of cash, and distribution of cocaine was broken and replaced by more professional independent radio promoters. A new generation of indies, most notably Jeff McClusky, developed the comparably expensive but much more palatable business practice that prevailed during the 1990s of gift exchange centered around support for station promotional campaigns rather than quid pro quos for cash and drugs pocketed by program directors. One measure of the extent of these changes is that while the 2005 scandal revealed that record labels were still compensating radio stations for airplay, at least they were finally doing so without using either drugs or the mob.

3.1.4 Corporate Radio, Professionalized Payola, and the 2005 Spitzer Investigation

The dramatic changes to the radio industry in the late 1990s form the back story to the 2005 payola scandal. The Telecommunications Act of 1996 (among other things) dramatically relaxed restrictions on the number of radio stations any one firm could own. This unleashed a wave of conglomeration and in 1999 Clear Channel merged with Jacor to achieve its current size as owning about a thousand radio stations at any given time, far larger than either its closest competitors or than was allowed prior to 1996.[24] Owning about a tenth of all commercial radio stations has helped make Clear Channel a favorite target for criticism by investigative journalists and the "media reform" social movement.[25] Thus, when Clear Channel attempted to institutionalize and rationalize payola, it did not go unnoticed.

In 2001, Clear Channel considered signing an exclusive chainwide deal with the independent radio promoter Tri State Promotions & Marketing, which was rumored to charge up to $1,000 for getting a song played on one station.[26] Having a single indie control access to a company that owned about one in ten American radio stations would give Tri State more market power and probably increase payola costs. Likewise, Clear Channel proposed charging for "back-announcing," which is when a disk jockey reads the song title and artist after a song has played. In January 2003, Senator Russ Feingold (D-WI) introduced the "Competition in Radio and Concert Industries Act" and held related hearings in the Commerce Committee. Several provisions were directly aimed at Clear Channel, which in addition to radio also had a near monopoly on concert promotion.[27] In part thanks to the regulatory threat and other criticism, Clear Channel almost immediately cut off all ties to independent radio promoters and in late 2005 spun off its concert promotion unit into an independent company called Live Nation. However, far from ending payola, Clear Channel's shunning of indies appears to have had the effect of driving record labels to more brazen direct promotion practices. As the state of New York discovered, the labels lacked the tact to practice payola as discreetly as had the indies.

As with the 1959 Kefauver investigation and the 1973 drugola scandal, the New York state investigation grew out of an earlier investigation. New York State Attorney General Eliot Spitzer made a practice of investigating corporations and extracting consent decrees that effectively established new regulatory regimes, and the strength of this record got him elected governor (although a prostitution scandal kept his tenure short). In 2004, Spitzer's office was investigating the failure of record companies to properly pay out royalties to artists (whom the labels claimed they were unable to locate). Because promotional expenses are deducted from royalties, this naturally led Spitzer's office to the issue of payola, particularly at the Entercom Contemporary Hits Radio station WKSE-FM in Buffalo. In 2004 alone, WKSE-FM raised $93,000 in payola (not including the hard to quantify value of live performances). In November 2004, the state subpoenaed records and between July 2005 and June 2006, it signed consent decrees with Sony BMG music, Warner Music Group, Universal Music Group, EMI Music North America, CBS Radio, and Entercom Communications. These firms account for the overwhelming majority of record sales and a healthy minority of radio stations. The consent decrees all required the firms to make charitable donations and abide by a series of restrictions on business practices, such as reporting to the monitored airplay databases when songs are played as part of advertising time (such as sponsored "showcase" programs). In April 2007, the FCC released the "Rules of Engagement," its own set of consent decrees with Clear Channel, CBS, Entercom, and Citadel which required these leading radio chains to devote a quota of airplay to music on independent labels and to keep records of label gifts which would be open to FCC audits.

Perhaps the most interesting result of the 2005 payola scandal were the many subpoenaed documents appended to the New York consent decrees showing how payola worked. These documents were typically receipts or invoices filed by record company people and (in accordance with the post-1986 system) ultimately billable to the band as "recoupable debt" against royalties. Less often they were discussions between record company people of promotional strategies. Relatively few of the documents are e-mails between radio stations and record company people. Presumably such negotiations mostly occur on the phone or in person, but they can nonetheless be inferred when the record company person invoices the transaction.

Many of the documents describe giving gifts to radio stations. The gift may be provided with only an expectation of future reciprocity, which makes it a true gift in the technical sense used by social scientists. As in other spheres, the in-kind form, the tactful avoidance of directly discussing reciprocity, the asynchronous achievement of reciprocity, and a rather loose and flexible accounting of whether reciprocity is achieved all obscure the underlying transactional aspect of a gift exchange relationship.[28] Sometimes these gifts can be things like a sound board or office equipment, but the vast majority of the time such gifts are tied to the station's own promotional campaigns to attract and retain listeners. For instance, when a DJ announces on the air that the tenth caller will get concert tickets, that prize was almost always a gift from a record label. A special case of in-kind gifts is "showola," where bands perform for free on the air or at concerts staged by the station. While these gifts usually go to promotional expenses, over the long run they are fungible with the station's general revenues as stations learn to keep lean promotional budgets since they can depend on continuous support from record labels to achieve this function.

Note the irony that in radio the recent shift away from the cash nexus and toward gift exchange is seen as an advance for professionalism rather than backsliding into patrimonialism, even though arms-length money-based quid pro quo exchange is typically seen as a defining characteristic of modernity.[29] Newer promoters like Jeff McClusky, who facilitate gift exchange, are universally seen as more professional than the older "Network" promoters, who mostly relied on cash. This is because even in modern economies, there are strong cultural and legal norms as to which goods and services can form an exchange circuit (i.e., legitimately be exchanged for one another).[30] The exchange of cash for airplay is prohibited by laws against payola and stigmatized by the romantic ideology of artistic creativity. As such, professionalism consists of finding ways to legitimate the exchange not by rationalizing it, but by obfuscating it so as to keep from spoiling the interaction.

In those e-mails that directly involve the radio station, the tone is often of a friendly gift exchange where exchange is in-kind and reciprocity is only implicit. For instance, in several e-mails, Mike Danger of WZNE maintained a friendly tone and used rhetoric consistent with mutually beneficial long-term partnership, as when he wrote to an EMI official:

> I need a favor...
>
> Carson and I are planning a trip to NYC to visit labels and we need air and hotel. We'd like to fly out on 1/29 and return on 2/1. Can you hook us up?
>
> I promise to say good things about you in front of [REDACTED].
> MD

The EMI promotional person likewise treated the request as part of an embedded tie and merely asked for arrival and departure time, without specifying exactly what WZNE would be expected to do in return.

In other cases the programmers are much more aggressive and blunt, most notoriously WKSE programmer Dave Universal, who eschewed the use of indies and would explicitly negotiate the dollar value of airplay directly with record labels and treat the label's debt to him as an expense account. Universal went so far as to repeatedly demand payment and to threaten to blacklist a label's artists. Of course at times the labels also bargained aggressively. For instance, WBLI promised to play EMI artists in exchange for travel to the Video Music Awards and when the label realized that they were only being played once a day, a label official felt cheated and asked a subordinate:

> Do they have their tickets yet? Do they have their flight shit done? I mean we can cancel the travel portion. I really don't give a rat's ass.

Likewise, EMI decided to stiff WSTW when it discovered that the station wasn't playing N.E.R.D. as frequently as the label felt was implied by their deal.

In almost three out of four documents, the record label is providing an in-kind gift. About half of the time this gift is concert tickets (sometimes including travel to the concert and not always for the band being promoted) and the other half of the time it is consumer electronics such as iPods or video games. In a minority of cases the gift is swag, often autographed by the band. The usual assumption is that these gifts will be passed on to listeners, but in some cases it is ambiguous whether they will be retained by station staff. Indeed, in an e-mail offering bribes to 13 programmers, a promotional person at Universal offered great specificity about the terms of the quid pro quo but was explicitly indifferent as to whether the gift would be used for a listener contest or the programmers' personal use:

> Six-0 Gotta Go!
>
> If your station adds and accumulates 60 spins on Pat Green's "Guy Like Me" by Sunday midnight, February 29, according to Mediabase...
>
> We will fly a station staff member plus one guest, -or- a winner plus a guest to ANY Pat Green show in the United States that is agreed upon. (Sold-out shows and private shows excluded.)
>
> One hotel night stayover, unless otherwise agreed
>
> 2 roundtrip tickets

33

> 2 show tickets
> 2 meet & greet passes
> 2 merchandise items
> 1 box of Pat Green albums for qualifying
> 2 additional albums for those attending shows

In other cases it is clear that gifts are being retained by the station staff, as when Warner Brothers paid $680 to send the staff of WSPK to dinner (on behalf of the Donnas) or $150 to buy a mini-fridge for WARQ (on behalf of My Chemical Romance). Likewise, two Virgin record officials venting about Dave Universal's avarice mentioned that Dave requested that Virgin Records not mention the deals to his own colleagues as "these deals are between Dave and Virgin."

In about 15 percent of the documents, the record label simply paid cash for spins. Sometimes this was as a time buy or showcase, where the station buys advertising time to play the music. Such a practice is legal as long as there is an on-air disclosure along the lines of "this is a paid advertisement" or "this song was brought to you by Universal Music Group." More often, though, the money goes through indies and is not disclosed on the air. For instance, between May and September of 2004, EMI devoted $76,499 to marketing the rock band Pillar, and almost all of that money went to indies, who billed $300 to $1,000 for each station that added the band to its playlist. In one case a label that made payment directly (rather than through an indie) decided to conceal the payment as "website support," before stopping to wonder whether the radio station actually had a website.

About 10 percent of the documents involved "showola" or concerts hosted by radio stations with tickets given to listeners and the performance usually broadcast on the air. Sometimes showola involves sending the bands to perform at the station concert, but just as often it is simply underwriting the concert.

In about 3 percent of the documents, the record labels dispense with honest graft and simply try to scam the radio stations with "phoner" campaigns. In these campaigns, labels hire telemarketers or indies and have them call in four or five times a day to request a song. On at least six different occasions, Universal Music Group used phoners in campaigns ranging in scope from 117 stations on behalf of Ludacris to a campaign devoted entirely to the MTV program *Total Request Live* on behalf of Lindsay Lohan. These campaigns were so thoroughly planned as to demand that the age, race, and gender of the callers match the demographics of the station's actual listeners. The manipulation of request lines by phoners is an open secret. Indies list these services on their websites, and radio stations are appropriately skeptical of requests and often ask follow-up questions to try to suss out whether a caller is a genuine listener.

3.2 Suppressing Payola

Of course, the New York state payola investigation was not primarily a data collection effort but an exercise of public policy intended to reduce the prevalence of payola in radio. To consider the investigation on its own terms, it is worth considering whether the New York and FCC settlements were successful in changing the business model of the music industry. A 2008 survey of independent record labels conducted by their trade group, A2IM, found most members reporting that payola had "decreased significantly in recent years" but that one in four had been approached about paying payola *since* the settlements, and about half said IRPs were still important to airplay.[31] Further evidence is difficult to come by because payola is surreptitious by nature and so there is a severe reflexivity problem in trying to measure the effects of exposure and criticism.

While only police work, witness testimony, and subpoenas can conclusively demonstrate a particular instance of payola, statistical analysis can help us estimate its prevalence over time. The purpose of payola is to allow record labels to co-opt radio airplay. While record labels have other, more legitimate, ways to influence broadcasting, payola is part of their portfolio of tactics and presumably has some marginal effect in helping record labels control radio airplay. In other words, when payola is common, record labels have more control over song selection and, conversely, song selection is relatively exogenous to the system of radio stations. Diffusion patterns differ dramatically depending on whether growth is endogenous or exogenous to the system of adopters and thus payola should be reflected by an especially exogenous pattern. In fact, comparison of songs mentioned in the documents subpoenaed by the New York state investigation against a comparable control sample showed that songs known to have involved payola do have the expected pattern of especially exogenous diffusion curves.[32] This implies that even without direct documentary evidence of payola, its prevalence can be inferred by analyzing the diffusion of songs. Unlike relying on documentary evidence, this indirect approach escapes the problems of reflexivity and temporal sparseness.

To estimate the sensitivity of payola to the policy shock of the 2005 scandal, I collected a sample of 1,137 songs released between 2002 and 2007.[33] For each of these songs I identify how many stations began playing the song per week and use this as the basis of a multilevel diffusion curve (MDC) analysis. This technique combines information on the diffusions of many innovations to identify patterns in what *sorts* of innovations tend to diffuse by which patterns.[34] In this case I analyzed the data to create a time series of diffusion patterns to examine the effect of the policy shock. Or rather, to examine the set of policy shocks, as the most recent payola scandal was not a single event but a series of related events unfolding along the following timeline:

- January 2003—Senator Feingold reintroduces "Competition in Radio and Concert Industries Act" and holds Commerce Committee hearings
- March 2003—Clear Channel cuts ties to independent radio promoters
- October 2004—New York Attorney General subpoenas record label documents
- July 2005–June 2006—Each of the four major record labels signs a consent decree with the New York Attorney General
- October 2006–December 2006—New York Attorney General signs consent decrees with CBS and Entercom radio chains
- April 2007—Federal Communication Commission signs the "rules of engagement" consent decrees with Clear Channel and three other large radio chains

Using MDC, I constructed a time series shown in figure 3.2 of how exogenous song diffusion curves were throughout this period.[35] When this metric is high it indicates that stations tended to adopt pop songs in a wave just after the initial release, whereas when the metric is low adoption tends to be less coupled to the release date. This pattern of an immediate batch of adoptions up front is consistent with a model where each actor in the system is responding to influence from outside the population of actors. Since the record industry is the most plausible source of exogenous influence on the song choices of radio, the metric can be interpreted as the degree to which the record industry has influence over radio.

This time-series analysis shows that diffusion patterns were generally similar throughout the period of the scandal, with a few exceptions. Most notably, there was a sharp (and brief) dip in the exogeneity co-efficient when the New York Attorney General subpoenaed documents and a smaller dip several months before the FCC reached its "rules of engagement" consent decrees with the four largest radio chains. This indicates that during these two periods, record labels were unwilling or unable to exert substantial pressure on the radio industry. The most likely cause for these brief relaxations of control are deterrence and regime uncertainty.

By 2004, New York Attorney General Spitzer had a reputation for aggressive but brief inquiries into white collar crime in various industries.

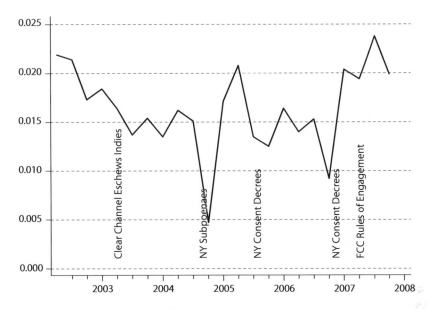

FIGURE 3.2. Exogenous Diffusion Coefficient by Quarter

Typically he would subpoena documents, issue press releases and leaks that tarnished companies' reputations (and often creditworthiness), and finally reach a consent decree in which the company neither confirms nor denies wrongdoing but agrees to make a charitable donation in lieu of a fine and abide by a new set of rules. Although Spitzer almost never actually brought cases to trial, his investigations themselves could be devastating. This threat of embarrassment was particularly acute for the radio and recorded music industries, as they desperately needed favorable policy environments: continued deregulation in the case of radio and aggressive intellectual property rights enforcement in the case of recorded music. Firms that are highly sensitive to the policy environment must be highly attuned to how legitimate they appear, and so public shaming by Spitzer was a severe threat.[36] Not surprisingly, when Spitzer first demanded documents the music industry appears to have panicked and perhaps ceased not only payola practices for which a court might find grounds for conviction, but also promotion practices that while perfectly legal could still be framed as shameful by a notoriously zealous prosecutor. Such a freeze-up is reflected by the almost zeroed-out rate of exogenous patterns of adoption immediately after the subpoenas.

Likewise, the last quarter of 2006 saw another drop in the capacity of the record industry to influence radio adoption patterns. Around

37

this time, members of the FCC began taking seriously the findings of the New York state investigation. In theory, radio stations do not own their broadcasting frequencies as freehold property but are only licensed to use them to serve the public interest. Therefore, technically payola is a violation of the licensee's trusteeship of public property and the FCC is responsible for policing such malfeasance. That the FCC had been upstaged by a state prosecutor implied a dereliction of duty, especially since Spitzer directed most of his attention to record labels and with a few exceptions did not demand reforms or fines directly from broadcasters. In particular, the two Democrats on the FCC, Michael Copps and Jonathan Adelstein, were sympathetic to the media reform movement and had previously expressed concern about the payola issue at events sponsored by the Future of Music Coalition. In late 2006, the New York state investigation was coming to a close with the signing of consent decrees with Entercom and CBS (as well as Spitzer's election as governor). This provided an opening for the FCC to launch its own investigation and set its own rules, in much the same way that from 1958 to 1960, the Kefauver Senate hearings, begat the Harris House hearings, which in turn begat hearings at the Federal Trade Commission and ultimately passage of an amendment to the Communications Act in Congress. There was a nontrivial threat that the FCC would take drastic action such as revoking broadcasting licenses of gross offenders (most obviously Entercom) or creating campaign-finance style bans of the exchange of anything of value between labels, indies, and stations to be backed up by regular audits tied to license renewal. As such, it behooved the music industry to walk the straight and narrow until the FCC closed the issue. Similarly, in 1986 the RIAA voted to break ties to indies just days after Giuliani subpoenaed evidence from them.

In all of these cases, trading patterns between the recording and broadcasting industries were disrupted by the realization of prosecutorial scrutiny and the proximate deterrence it implied. However, the key word is "proximate" as business models quickly reverted to something close to the status quo ante. Shortly after both the Spitzer subpoenas and the beginning of FCC interest in the scandal, the record industry reassumed its usual influence over radio, in both cases before the state even finalized its sanctions. In the case of the FCC inquiry, it quickly became apparent to informed observers that the FCC did not plan a harsh response to the payola issue, in part because Chairman Martin was extremely focused on the issue of cable television rates and did not want to be distracted for the remainder of his term by making payola a high priority. Therefore, well before the FCC actually issued its "rules of engagement," it became clear to the music industry that the FCC intended to reach a negotiated light solution rather than an imposed harsh one. Likewise, Spitzer was known for inquiries that were severe but not sustained, and thus after the subpoenas it was likely that he would not further scrutinize the industry.

The most interesting case is the 1986 response, in which the radio and record industries did make permanent changes to the details of the payola business model, but within a few years had reestablished something functionally equivalent in broad outline. Prior to 1986, payola was funneled through a cartel of indies connected to organized crime who claimed stations as territory and compensated program directors with cash and cocaine. More recently, a station is usually not exclusively represented by one indie, there is free entry into the indie market, the indies are respectable and professional and they tend to operate by developing gift exchange relationships with stations using in-kind gifts that mostly go to benefit the stations' own promotional campaigns. While these details were substantially different from (and almost certainly preferable to) the old system, the end result is the same: resources are flowing from the record industry to the radio industry in order to affect the choice of songs for airplay. Furthermore, while it is difficult to make a precise estimate, the volume of trade appears to be comparable. For instance, Dannen (1990) provides estimates for the independent radio promotion budget of a single as ranging from $100,000 up to $300,000 under the old system, in the early 1980s. In 1998, under the new system, it cost about $350,000 in independent radio promoter billings to get the song "Closing Time" substantial airplay in Alternative, Top 40, and Adult Contemporary.[37] Controlling for inflation, Slichter's figure is right in the middle of Dannen's range. Since "Closing Time" was a reasonably popular song but never reached the top ten, this implies that the Jeff McClusky model of providing in-kind support for station promotional campaigns is more subtle but just as expensive as the Joe Isgro model of stuffing cash in record sleeves. This should not be surprising, as it is common for an industry to reconstitute itself in response to regulatory threat in ways that obey the letter of the law but evade the basic motivation.[38] The regime uncertainty of active government involvement may disrupt trade, but once the punishments are doled out and the rules are rewritten, the market reestablishes itself in a new form.

3.2.1 The Robust Logic of Payola

The most fundamental question is *why* the payola market continually reestablishes itself and *who* benefits from the system.[39] This question is best answered by considering a starting point where payola does not exist, either because it has recently been purged or because we posit a hypothetical state of nature relationship between Crusoe Records and Friday Broadcasting. In such a situation, radio programmers are choosing songs based only on their best estimate of their appeal to listeners. In some cases they will consider a song and reject it. This is frustrating to the person responsible for promoting this song, and it may occur to them that if the intrinsic merits of the song are less than the competition, they can sweeten the deal with a little payola.

It makes sense for stations to accept this payola if they expect that the value of the bribe is greater than the loss of advertising dollars implied by the drop in ratings (if any) that will follow from deviating from the playlist they would construct only with regard to audience interest.[40] The model is slightly more complicated but largely comparable if payola is directed to station staff rather than directly to the bottom line. In theory it might present a principle-agent problem for the station staff to benefit while, on the margin, decreasing station ratings. However, when payola is an accepted business practice it can be an implicit part of compensation which is fungible with direct station expenditures, and may even be preferable for management as it evades taxes, places the risk of variable revenues on the staff rather than the station, and avoids monitoring costs. Although it is difficult to prove this model in modern radio, it was definitely the case in vaudeville and early radio when performers would often have little or no salary and were expected to earn an income on kickbacks from Tin Pan Alley publishers.[41] Likewise, it is worth noting that before the first payola scandal, station management tended to take a "boys will be boys" approach to payola. When stations nowadays instigate payola investigations of their own staff, the motive appears to be avoiding state sanctions rather than maximizing ratings through preserving the integrity of their playlist.

In any case, it's unlikely that a radio station would be asked to take a bribe to play a really unappealing record, since a reasonable record label wouldn't want to waste money promoting music that they know to be terrible.[42] Of course if a station prefers song A, but accepts a dollar to replace it with B, then song A will not be played, even though it is the best choice on the merits (albeit perhaps only by a small margin). The owners of song A may make a counter-offer of two dollars, and the price will escalate from there. At this point, payola is no longer a sweetener used to induce consideration of marginal songs, but a mandatory part of business even for songs that are intrinsically very appealing. A bidding war for airplay breaks out and this eventually leads to rent dissipation, with the cost of payola equaling the marginal benefit of airplay and this cost being so high that nearly all profits from the recording industry are captured by broadcasting. At this point the volume of the illicit payola market attracts the interest of the state and/or the recording industry grows frustrated and attempts collective action. Whether by state or by trade group, such a response temporarily suppresses payola and brings the system full circle.

Indeed, this stylized model closely matches the historical facts and helps explain why—like a cicada—every 15 years or so payola emerges from underground and becomes conspicuous. The need to control the publicity that drives record sales spurs record labels to co-opt radio stations. Since there is a finite amount of airplay, the record labels effectively get into bidding wars over it and eventually this behavior grows so egregious that it attracts the interest of the state or the labels themselves balk at the expense. Boycotts are temporarily honored or prosecutions temporarily terrify the industry into staying on the straight and narrow, and then the cycle of bribery begins anew.

The clearest illustration of the cyclical nature is the situation before and after the 1986 RIAA boycott of indies. In 1973, Columbia Records responded to the "drugola" scandal by purging David Wynshaw and Clive Davis and hiring an outside law firm to audit the company's involvement with drugs, organized crime, and payola. Within a few years, the situation had apparently reverted to type. In 1979, Dick Asher was transferred from an overseas stint to work as a vice president of CBS Records (the parent company of Columbia).[43] He discovered that the company had low margins on high sales in large part because it was spending $10 million a year on independent radio promoters. As a cost-cutting experiment he refused to pay indies to promote Pink Floyd's single "Another Brick in the Wall" to Los Angeles radio stations, reasoning that promotion oughtn't be necessary for a song that was already a hit and which came from a best-selling album and was being supported by an extremely successful concert tour. In fact, none of the four Top 40 stations in Los Angeles would play the song. Asher interpreted this as evidence that paying indies was not a consulting service but payola and the system was so strong that it did not influence radio so much as control it, with payola being effectively a compulsory tax. Pink Floyd's management's interpretation was much more pragmatic; the band needed to get on the radio and if paying the tax was necessary, then CBS better pay it.

The next year, David Horowitz at Warner Brothers reached a similar reading of the balance sheet and decided to boycott the use of independent radio promoters, with CBS joining in a few months later.[44] These decisions faced resistance from label heads (i.e., middle management) at both Warner and CBS, who felt that this placed them at a competitive disadvantage, and *Billboard* reported that Atlantic, a Warner subsidiary, simply ignored the policy. In response to this boycott, the Network gave another *example par les autres* performance by blacklisting Loverboy (one of Asher's pet projects at CBS) and the Who (one of Warner's most reliable acts). Again, artist management pressured record executives to appease the indies and developed work-arounds with the label heads to circumvent the ban for the few months it took for Asher and Horowitz to come to reason and resume paying the Network.

The next attempt at breaking payola came in 1986, after Giuliani subpoenaed record label documents regarding the Network. This time the major labels presented a united front through the RIAA and had the power of constraint in that the Network understood that the labels feared public association with the mob and possible prosecution. This credible and united opposition broke the Network and reduced the volume of payola down to trivial levels. However, the interesting thing is that the industry could not maintain a low payola equilibrium.

Almost immediately following the RIAA's ban on direct interaction with indies, artists and artist managers began seeking a competitive advantage and using payola to attain it. In a few cases, established and cash-rich artists would pay the expenses out-of-pocket, but the business model quickly developed that the label would loan this money to the artist as "tour support" to be recoupable against future royalties. Of course this meant that artists kept less of the royalties, but they were willing to do so for greater airplay and eventually they entered an arms race with other artists where this was not a competitive advantage but a necessary baseline expense. As described above, by the late 1990s (if not earlier), the expense (if not the form) of payola was comparable to that in the early 1980s. This should not be surprising since in a market the price of a fixed quantity resource tends to be bid up to its value. Payola was just as expensive in the 1990s as the 1980s because it was just as important for record sales.

Thus, payola is something that begins as a bribe paid by labels and artists, but can quickly end up as extortion demanded by broadcasters. A particular record company can benefit tremendously if it provides payola and its rivals do not, for this company will not only have a great advantage in promoting its products, but will pay a low price for doing so. However, once payola becomes universal all the record companies pay a high price and have no net promotion advantage for doing so. This incentive structure is the familiar prisoner's dilemma, where an actor's best outcome is to cheat while its partner behaves, followed by them both behaving, followed by them both cheating, and worst of all is for the actor to behave while its partner cheats. Since for any given partner action, the actor's greatest payoff is for cheating, the dominant strategy is to cheat. Unfortunately this means that most of the time both of them will cheat and such mutual defection has a dismal joint payoff. In the case of the record industry, this means little or no aggregate gain in promotional exposure and with rent dissipation diverting much of their profits to broadcasters.[45]

The only solution to the prisoner's dilemma is collective action over repeated interaction, but even this is tenuous. In essence, rather than buying a scarce resource and bidding up the price, record companies could agree with each other to refuse to pay for the resource. In this light, it makes sense that Joe Isgro sued the major record labels for forming a combination in restraint of trade after the RIAA voted to stop paying bribes to the Network. The RIAA's action was in fact a textbook case of a monopsonistic cartel, though the absurdity of Isgro's suit is that the market they agreed to stay out of is itself illegal. Unfortunately for musicians and the record industry, cartels are extremely vulnerable to cheating (especially when monitoring is unfeasible because the behavior at issue is surreptitious) and thus it's not surprising that the prisoner's dilemma reached its usual unpleasant equilibrium.

Indeed, the issue of escalating promotion costs and the ineffectual collective action efforts of firms to limit them is an old one. Similar practices known as "song plugging" were pervasive during the vaudeville era, when the basic business model was not the sale of recorded music promoted by broadcasting but the sale of sheet music promoted through live performances. As with payola, bidding wars broke out and began to swallow the earnings of composers and the profits of publishers. To solve this situation, in 1917 the various Tin Pan Alley publishers and *Variety* magazine formed the Music Publishers Protective Association.[46] The explicit goal of the trade association was to get its members to eschew bribing stage performers. Although this was self-regulation and the promotion medium at issue was the stage, not the airwaves, the goal was similar to that of the various attempts by the state since 1960 to keep a lid on payola in broadcasting. However, the publishers almost immediately reneged on their promises to one another to eschew bribes and let the music speak for itself. In hindsight, it's not surprising that Music Publishers Protective Association failed to eradicate payola in 1917 when we know that similar attempts at collective action in 1981 and 1986 failed, and even the state (with its power to subpoena, fine, and jail) could not accomplish the feat either in 1960, 1973, or 1990. While it is too early to say conclusively whether payola will survive the aftermath of the 2005 scandal, historical precedent and basic logic suggest that it is a permanent feature of the music industry.

4

CAN RADIO STATIONS BREAK SINGLES?

As seen in chapter 3, record labels are tremendously interested in getting radio stations to play their songs. As described in that chapter, record labels will go to great lengths to promote their songs to stations, going so far as to pay for the privilege (often in roundabout and genteel ways). However, record labels are not interested in all stations equally. Some stations are seen as keystones to an entire format with the ability to "break" a single.[1] The consensus is that while any station can be first to play a single, only certain high-status stations can *cause* a single to disseminate to other stations.[2] For instance, KROQ-FM of Los Angeles has long been considered the most important station in the "Alternative" or "Modern Rock" format. In his memoir, the drummer from Semisonic describes what it was like to have KROQ break his single "Closing Time":

> "K-Rock is adding the single."
>
> It was Jim [Semisonic's manager], savoring my disbelief at such spectacular news. To be added to the playlist of Los Angeles-based KROQ ("K-ROCK") is to be anointed by the ruling superpower of alternative-rock radio. This was a resounding endorsement, one that would reverberate throughout the world of radio. Over the course of our previous album, K-ROCK had ignored us completely, but now they made a dramatic turnabout. As one of the K-ROCK executives said to an MCA higher-up, "We want to make Semisonic our band."[3]

This belief in the special influence of KROQ over other Alternative rock stations is not idiosyncratic to Semisonic, but is widespread among other people responsible for promoting rock music:

> Kelso Jacks of Roadrunner Records states that record companies often press the envelope because they know some PDs look to see what other stations are playing before adding a record. "There are the taste-maker stations that everyone else in the country is looking at to see their playlist. K-Rock in Los Angeles—if they add something to their regular rotation modern rock programmers across the country are saying *Ooohh! Maybe I should add that record too, because those guys are hot.*"[4]

The station's fame goes back to the late 1970s and early 1980s when disk jockey Rodney "on the ROQ" Bingenheimer was widely seen as a key figure for importing British music and nurturing similar local acts, most notably being the first American disk jockey to play the Sex Pistols, as well as being an early supporter of Los Angeles punk bands like X and Black Flag.[5] The station's fame built in the 1980s and 1990s as first new wave and later punk became important strains in rock music. CBS Radio (KROQ's parent company) has attempted to leverage this special status for the station across the chain by making the program director, Kevin Weatherly, a senior vice president and the architect of the "Adult Hits" format (which goes by the brand name "Jack FM"), all while also keeping him at KROQ.

4.1 The Role of "Opinion Leaders" in Diffusion

The idea that a small number of prestigious radio stations like KROQ set the agenda for entire radio formats is just a special case of the "opinion leadership" diffusion hypothesis. This chapter will first review this concept in order to derive several empirical implications from the model. I will then show that radio meets the network structure scope conditions for the hypothesis but nonetheless fails to show opinion leadership on a consistent basis. Finally, I examine "My Humps," a song that presents an especially favorable test of the hypothesis.

The opinion leadership concept dates back to the "two-step flow" model which was first formulated in the context of the 1940 presidential election.[6] This study found that most voters were not especially influenced by the mass media but rather by key members of their peer group. The mass media had an indirect effect because these opinion leaders themselves garnered information and ideas from mass media. A follow-up study found that opinion leaders exist in many fields, but their expertise is often specific such that, for instance, one member of a peer group might be relied upon for advice on consumer goods, another on politics, and a third about films.[7]

These themes were picked up in Rogers's *Diffusion of Innovations*, which has been through five editions between 1962 and 2003 and is widely used as an undergraduate and graduate text. The book treats hybrid corn as the paradigmatic case and emphasizes endogenous processes, especially direct interpersonal influence (as compared to general cascades). Instead of using event history regression analyses, Rogers divides actors by adoption time into several ideal types. The key actors in contagion are the "early adopters" (roughly the 3rd through 15th percentile by adoption time), who Rogers describes as being qualitatively different from the "innovators" (the first 2 percentiles by adoption time). Although the innovators are the first to adopt an innovation, they are not especially important to its diffusion because they are less connected to their local communities than to a translocal community of tinkerers, hackers, and gadget aficionados. In contrast, the early adopters are key:

> Early adopters are a more integrated part of the local social system than are innovators. Whereas innovators are cosmopolites, early adopters are localites. This adopter category, more than any other, has the highest degree of opinion leadership in most systems. Potential adopters look to early adopters for advice and information about an innovation. The early adopter is considered by many to be "the individual to check with" before adopting a new idea. This adopter category is generally sought by change agents as a local missionary for speeding the diffusion process. Because early adopters are not too far ahead of the average individual in innovativeness, they serve as a role model for many other members of a social system. Early adopters help trigger the critical mass when they adopt an innovation.[8]

Thus, early adopters are those who have sufficient influence to make an innovation tip. Although this is somewhat tautological, since "early adopters" are defined as those who adopt just before tipping, Rogers argues that they have systematic characteristics such as a central network position and above-average wealth and intelligence. He provides evidence that early adopters tend to be opinion leaders from studies of pesticides among farmers and math pedagogy among school superintendents. As implied by the book's frequent references to "change agents," one of the implications of a causal role for these key actors is that there may be a practical benefit to co-opting them. Although

Rogers was primarily interested in public health officials using local opinion leaders to disseminate health behaviors, drug companies have long tried to identify and co-opt influential doctors, and more recently general marketers have become interested in identifying and co-opting influential consumers.[9]

One of the strongest pieces of evidence for a special role of highly connected people came from a chain letter experiment in which hundreds of people in Nebraska and Boston were asked to reach a particular investor in Boston via friends of friends. A quarter of the chains ultimately reached the target, with those originating in Boston requiring an average of 4.4 intermediaries and those originating in Nebraska, 5.7 intermediaries. Rounding up the latter figure is the origin of the famous "six degrees of separation" factoid.[10] Most relevant to the opinion leadership hypothesis is that certain people appeared in multiple successful chains. In particular, there were three people who appeared in, respectively, 16, 10, and 5 of the 64 completed chains. The researchers' interpretation was that certain people act as highly central "sociometric stars" (aka, social network hubs) who are key to connecting the network. Subsequent research has confirmed that most social networks do indeed feature tremendous variance in the distribution of connectedness, with a few actors being massively more connected than average.[11]

Currently, the opinion leadership hypothesis is closely associated with the journalist Malcolm Gladwell, whose article "The Coolhunt" and best-selling book *The Tipping Point* popularized social science on diffusion and made him into a much sought management guru.[12] In the book Gladwell describes social epidemics of the sort that result from an endogenous hazard function, where the likelihood of someone adopting the innovation is a function of how many people already have. Much of Gladwell's emphasis is on the special role played in diffusion by those people who are unusually well connected. He illustrates this premise by describing several exceptionally gregarious people of his acquaintance as well as drawing from the epidemiology literature to describe the allegedly key role in sexually transmitted disease epidemics played by a few fantastically promiscuous people, like Gaëtan Dugas, the "patient zero" for HIV in the West. One of Gladwell's more interesting demonstrations is the enormous variance in responses he gets when he administers the "phone book test" in which he has asked people to check how many surnames they recognize from a representative list.[13] Gladwell infers that these especially connected people (whom he describes as "connectors") are the key drivers of diffusion. The practical implication of this argument is the "viral marketing" strategy, which became popular in large part because of

Gladwell's book. In this strategy one does not aim to convince all consumers indiscriminately, but rather to identify the influentials and convince them, then let the influentials convince the mass public for you. This strategy is seen in extreme form with the Twitter analytics firm Klout and Microsoft's patent #US20090307073, both of which involve algorithms to identify opinion leaders and offer them discounted or free products in the hopes that they will pass along their impressions of the product to their direct and indirect followers.

The strong form of the opinion leadership hypothesis can be taken to mean that highly connected actors are not just disproportionately important to diffusion, but the key to it. However, this model is controversial in the academic literature. An e-mail-based replication of the "six degrees" chain letter experiment found that highly connected hubs were not especially important to completing chains.[14] A meta-analysis of several empirical diffusion studies found a consistent effect that highly connected people tend to be early adopters of successful innovations, though the study remained agnostic as to whether there is a causal relationship.[15] Computer simulations and formal models have suggested that even highly connected actors are only marginally important to diffusion. Overall the most important determinants of diffusion are simply the intrinsic appeal of the innovation and the distribution of individual thresholds for adoption.[16] Social network effects are contingent on the thresholds, with intrinsically appealing innovations spreading most rapidly through weak ties and intrinsically unappealing innovations spreading most effectively through cliquish networks.[17] Since, by definition, most of the ties of highly connected actors are weak ties, this implies that they can only be effective at promoting diffusion for intrinsically appealing innovations; however, such innovations can usually be promoted more effectively through exogenous means or simply the endogenous process of the general level of adoption. Thus, the strong form of the opinion leadership hypothesis only works in simulation under an implausible combination of assumptions.

4.2 The Distribution of Connection in Radio

Regardless of what social network scientists think about the issue in theory, people in the music industry believe that opinion leader radio stations are key to the diffusion of pop songs. Furthermore, it is worth noting that the qualitative evidence cited above about widespread belief in the special role of stations like KROQ predates the publication of *The Tipping Point*. We might then suspect that this reflects real knowledge about how radio works rather than just being a performativity effect—the result of the music industry being taken up in the viral marketing

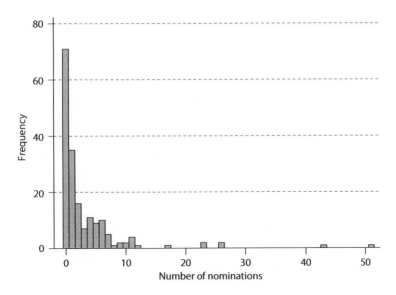

FIGURE 4.1. Distribution of Nominations for Top 40 Stations

business fad. It is thus worth seriously examining the evidence for the opinion leadership hypothesis in radio. The opinion leadership hypothesis has two major empirical implications. First, that some actors are especially central to the social network. Second, that diffusion is very sensitive to the adoption behavior of these highly central actors.

To test these implications, I conducted a survey of stations in the Top 40 format. See appendix A for details on this survey. The key set of questions in the survey was to create a directed social network of radio stations. This allows me to see how popular each station was with its peers as well as specific pathways through which contagious diffusion might occur.

Figure 4.1 shows the distribution of Top 40 stations by their popularity among their peers. There are 181 Top 40 stations eligible for nomination and a total of 421 nominations, or an average of 2.33 nominations per eligible station.[18] However, the nominations were not allocated evenly, with most stations being unpopular and a handful of stations being massively popular. First note that 99 stations were not nominated by any peers and 30 stations were nominated by only one peer. Thus, 71 percent of Top 40 stations are almost or entirely obscure to their peers, and their behavior is noticed only in the aggregate, via the pop charts. In contrast, the two most popular stations in the data set, WHTZ of New York and KIIS of Los Angeles, were each nominated

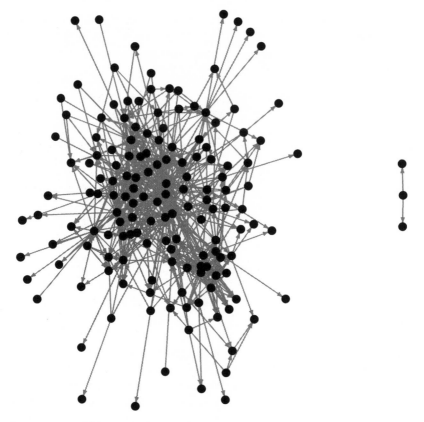

FIGURE 4.2. Social Network of Top 40 Stations

A directed tie between two stations reflects the station at the base of the arrow claiming to pay attention to the station at the point of the arrow. Attention need not be reciprocated. Attention was measured in a survey that asked programmers what other stations they listen to on the air, read about in trade magazines or monitored airplay databases, or with whose programmer they converse. The graph uses the Fruchterman-Reingold layout algorithm so that proximity in the graph reflects proximity in the social network

by more than 40 peers. Since programmers at 123 stations responded to the survey, this indicates that these two stations each attract the attention of at least one out of three Top 40 radio stations. While WHTZ and KIIS clearly dominate, such stations as WFLZ of Tampa, WNCI of Columbus, KDWB of Minneapolis, and KHKS of Dallas form a second tier of stations, getting about 20 nominations each.

This scale-free distribution of nominations is typical of networks and an important precondition for the opinion leadership hypothesis.[19] The plausibility of a special role for these stations can be seen by graphing the social network, as is done in figure 4.2. This graph (which uses the igraph library's implementation of the Fruchterman-Reingold algorithm) shows a core-periphery structure dominated by a few stations like KIIS and WHTZ.[20] As can be seen, the vast majority of stations are reachable from this core, usually with a path length of just one or two. In other words, most stations are either attentive to WHTZ or KIIS or attentive to another station that is itself attentive to these popular stations. Thus, we could imagine that were KIIS or WHTZ to add a song, this might be noticed by almost 50 stations, and if these stations imitated this behavior, the song would in turn be noticed by the stations that admire them. It is thus prima facie plausible that KIIS or WHTZ could be sufficiently influential that their behavior could set the agenda for the Top 40 format as a whole in much the same way that we saw described above for KROQ in the Modern Rock format.

4.3   Diffusion of Pop Songs and Radio Stations

Of course the opinion leadership hypothesis does not merely imply that some actors are especially popular (which, as we have seen, is indeed the case for radio), but that this popularity effectively translates into a powerful role in diffusion. That is, it is one thing to show that KIIS and WHTZ are especially admired and another to show that one of these stations adding a song will *cause* the song to become popular with other stations. If the imprimatur of a particular station did cause a song to be popular, we would expect that station to routinely begin playing hit pop songs earlier than other stations for the simple reason that once the station begins playing it, other stations follow and it becomes a hit. We would therefore expect to see an association between how popular a station is with its peers and how early it adopted songs that proved to be hits.[21]

Figure 4.3 displays a scatterplot of peer nominations against typical add dates.[22] The two most popular stations with their peers, WHTZ and KIIS, are labeled and they are entirely typical in their adoption times, despite their overwhelming advantage in peer nominations. WHTZ tends to adopt slightly later than the typical station and KIIS to adopt slightly earlier, but both stations have a wide range of add times (relative to the median) and quite commonly adopt well before or well after the bulk of stations. Under the opinion leadership theory we would expect to see highly central actors in the network usually having adoption times between negative two and negative one standard deviations.[23] This graph implies that we should expect to see KIIS and WHTZ around seven to fourteen days before the median rather than, as is the case, three or four days before or after the herd. Of the six stations

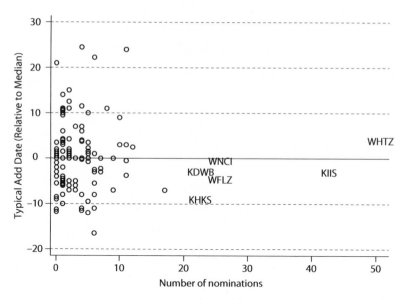

FIGURE 4.3. Typical Adoption Time as a Function of Nominations for Top 40 Stations

getting at least 20 peer nominations, only KHKS has a typical adoption time consistent with the opinion leadership hypothesis.

Thus, prestigious stations do not seem to be driving diffusion. However, this oughtn't come as a surprise, as the opinion leadership diffusion model is a special case of the endogenous growth model. Under the opinion leadership model we would expect to see an s-curve, with slow diffusion until one of the key actors adopts, after which point there would be accelerating diffusion. In fact—as shown in chapter 2—pop songs do not generally follow s-curves but concave diffusion patterns typical of an exogenous force, which—as seen in chapter 3—is almost certainly the promotional efforts of record labels. If the opinion leadership hypothesis is saying that key stations adopt just before the system reaches the tipping point, then this cannot be true if *there is no tipping point*. In other words, if the opinion leadership hypothesis is a subset of the endogenous model, and the endogenous model is generally a poor fit for radio, then it follows naturally that the opinion leadership hypothesis should also generally be a poor fit for radio. But what about for those exceptional cases when radio stations are not taking their cues from the record labels, but are spreading music among themselves? Might not the influentials be important given the contingency that the record labels have not made diffusion overdetermined?

4.4   The Role of Influentials for Endogenous Diffusion

The hip-hop group Black Eyed Peas formed in 1995 and had lack-luster success until they recruited Fergie, formerly of the pop group Wild Orchid. The Peas' next album, 2003's *Elephunk*, was a break-out hit, reaching 14 on the *Billboard* 200 album chart and putting three singles on the airplay charts. While the album was charting, the band was nearly omnipresent, as satirized in a *Saturday Night Live* skit advertising the band's willingness to make personal ap-pearances, license, and endorsements. Most notably, Apple used the dancehall-inflected single "Hey Mama" in its original "silhouette" ad campaign for the iPod, and the NBA used a bowdlerized version of the single "Get Retarded" as its theme song. In 2005, the Peas followed up this success with the album *Monkey Business*. At the time, pop critics worldwide singled out one track as especially awful, and some of these critiques display more creative writing than the lyrics themselves:

- Worst of all is "My Humps," an interminable paean to female member Fergie's hind and front quarters. (*San Diego Union Tribune*)
- Sure, there are also a couple of massive clunkers like Fer-gie's cringe-inducing My Humps, an ode to her "lovely lady lumps." (And they say rock lyrics aren't poetry.) (*Toronto Sun*)
- Fergie also co-stars in the track most likely to live in infamy: it's called "My Humps," and it requires her to declare, "You love my lady lumps." Uh-oh. Sounds like someone may have just earned herself a singularly unpleasant new nickname. (*New York Times*)
- Wildly unsuccessful is the group's utilization of its newest member, Fergie, to function as an imitator of the hyper-sexual Kelis/Ciara archetype on "My Humps," which makes for one of the most embarrassing rap performances of the new millennium (sample lyric: "My hump (9x)/My lovely little lumps"). (*All Music Guide*)
- Unfortunately the arrangements are generally paper-thin, the production dull and lyrics that started as satires of booty and bling become wholehearted celebrations, exemplified by the abysmal My Humps. (*The Sun Herald*)
- "My Humps" is laughably bad, basically sounding like a copy of any of Ciara's last three singles. (*Fresno Bee*)
- [S]kip the insipid "My Humps." (*Los Angeles Times*)
- Female crooner Fergie who boosted Elephunk out of the hip hop morass seems lost in the shuffle and will be remembered

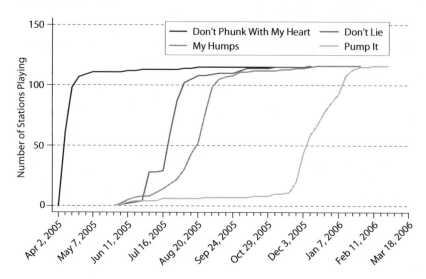

FIGURE 4.4. Diffusion Curves for Singles on the Black Eyed Peas Album *Monkey Business* on Top 40 Stations

> mostly for an embarrassing unimaginative bummer called "My Humps." (*Jerusalem Post*)

- If only they could write rhymes worth a damn. The asinine chorus to the Fergie showcase "My Humps" ("My humps/My lovely little baby humps") conjures up none of the erotic discomfiture that gave "Milkshake" and "Cameltoe" their bite. (*Village Voice*)

Universal Music Group, the Peas' record label, apparently had a similar assessment, as they passed over the song when choosing singles.

Just as with Rihanna's *Good Girl Gone Bad* (see chapter 2), Universal released and heavily promoted one single a few months before the album dropped, then planned to follow this up with a second single at the record release and a third a few months later. The first single was "Don't Phunk With My Heart" which they planned to follow with "Don't Lie" and "Pump It," keeping "My Humps" as an album cut indefinitely. However, as shown in figure 4.4, *Monkey Business* yielded a windfall hit. As noted in a *Slate* story decrying the song:

> The most fascinating aspect of "My Humps" is that it is widely believed to be the most successful unsolicited single in history, and, as of this writing, it is the most-downloaded song in the country. The Peas achieved all this without releasing a single. Instead, file sharers and intrepid radio

programmers were the ones who more or less discovered the song and pushed it toward hit status, eventually forcing the label to respond with a proper single release.[24]

"Don't Phunk With My Heart" was still receiving significant airplay when *Monkey Business* dropped on May 27 (and in fact "Phunk's" airplay would not peak until July), but as is typical, a second single began diffusing with the album's release. "Don't Lie" follows a fairly typical exogenous diffusion pattern of a sudden and rapid rise, consistent with aggressive record label promotion. At the same time, "My Humps" began to diffuse, but very gradually. In the first week of the album's release, two Top 40 stations began to play it, then another in the second week, and four in the third week.[25] The song continued to spread gradually for almost two months until it reached a tipping point at the end of July, at which point it began spreading rapidly among radio stations. In late August, Universal realized that it had three Black Eyed Peas songs on the charts (usually a band is lucky to have one or two charting singles) and hastily prepared a video, but by this point the song was already well on its way to saturating the Top 40 format.[26] So, contrary to the expectation of both Universal and most pop critics, "My Humps" became a hit. The most prescient review was probably that of *Rolling Stone*, which agreed with the consensus that the song was a "butt-stupid ode to Fergie's ass" but noted that it was an "*irresistible* butt-stupid ode to Fergie's ass" (emphasis added).

As discussed above, most songs almost by definition cannot show evidence for the opinion leadership hypothesis because their airplay is overdetermined by record label promotional efforts. In the case of "My Humps," we have a song that *did* follow an endogenous growth pattern and so a plausible test case for the effect of opinion leaders, given the contingency that peer influence is not swamped by exogenous diffusion pressures.

However, the timing of adoptions does not fit the pattern we would expect for an endogenous process where central actors were playing an influential role. As measured by the survey, the two stations held in greatest esteem by their peers were KIIS and WHTZ, therefore an opinion leadership model would expect the system to tip shortly after one or both of these stations adopted. The hazard rate for adopting "My Humps" rose gradually throughout July and rose quickly in the second week of August. If this diffusion were driven by strong opinion leaders, we would expect one or both of these stations to have adopted slightly before this tipping point, perhaps in the last week of July or first week of August. In fact, KIIS added the song on June 3, making it one of the first two stations to play the song (the other was WKFS of Cincinnati) and WHTZ was almost exactly at the median for Top 40 stations, adding the song on August 26. Consequently, of the two most plausible candidates for a strong influence role, one adopted after the tipping point and the other adopted far before it. KIIS appears to have been imitated by a handful of stations, but hardly to have driven the format all by itself. Rather than this being a case of the add by KIIS amounting to "My Humps" being "anointed by the superpower of [Top 40] radio," it seems that this add (and that of the less famous WKFS) started a snowball process and it was the accumulation of adds by many stations which helped it spread.

Indeed, it seems that not only is there no effect of the two highly central stations, but there is no effect of contagion more broadly. A model under which the most central stations cause the system to tip is based on the assumption that they cause their alters to adopt and their special role is because they have so many alters. The opinion leadership hypothesis is therefore just a special case of the contagion hypothesis; that ego's decision to adopt is a function of the alters' behavior. We can test this hypothesis with figure 4.5, which graphs the network graph again, but this time does so for selected dates with stations displayed as black if they had played "My Humps" as of that date.[27] For ease of reading the graph, the arcs are omitted from this version, but the layout algorithm makes it so that proximity in the graph is a good proxy for a network tie. Under the contagion hypothesis we would expect that the early dates would mostly see the black dots clustering in one part of the network, spreading out concentrically over time. Instead, we see the black dots appear randomly throughout the network. Many stations that began playing the song early are friendly with stations that played the song late, and vice versa. Thus, we must reject the idea that stations are basing their airplay decisions on particular peers and rivals, even given the scope condition that the record label promotional people are asleep at the wheel.

Nonetheless, as shown by the s-curve for "My Humps" in figure 4.4, there is an endogenous process. This seems paradoxical if one assumes that we are only aware of the behavior of those peers with whom we directly communicate. However, a little reflection shows that we may be aware of popularity in a general sense without associating adoption with particular alters. This sort of generalized awareness can even be more salient than the behavior of our specific alters. In pop music, this awareness of the general level of popularity occurs through the pop charts, and other cultural fields have comparable mechanisms for aggregating information.[28] Most radio programmers are closely attentive to the charts published in *Billboard* (and, until 2006, in *Radio & Records*). These charts aggregate the airplay of many stations and for the

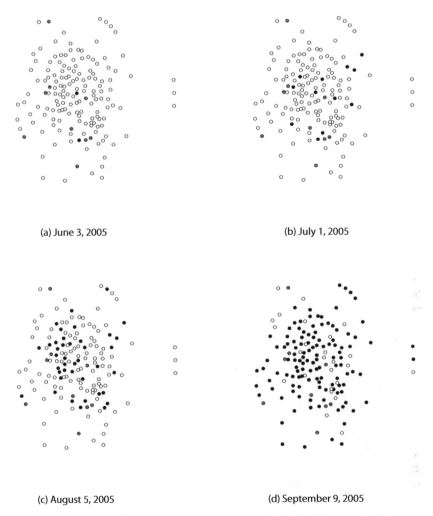

(a) June 3, 2005   (b) July 1, 2005

(c) August 5, 2005   (d) September 9, 2005

FIGURE 4.5. Top 40 Stations in Social Network Space with Filled Dots for Those Having Played "My Humps"
Note: Gray stations appear in social network data but not airplay data

most part do so without regard to the prestige or size of the station.[29] So the airplay of humble WZYP of Athens, Alabama has as much influence on the Top 40 chart as that of much-admired WHTZ of New York. In this way, both famous and obscure stations can have comparable influence on peers and will do so regardless of whether there is a direct social network tie between the stations.

57

Altogether, the opinion leadership hypothesis is a very poor fit for describing the diffusion of pop songs in radio. While there is a highly skewed distribution of station salience to peers, these highly connected stations are no more important to diffusion than are more obscure stations. So although the degree distribution of the radio station social network *is* consistent with the idea of opinion leaders, this hypothesis fails in every other way. First, the vast majority of pop songs are not really spread *between* radio stations but *to* radio stations. Second, even with the exceptional pop song that spreads endogenously, the mechanism appears to be a generalized cascade rather than cohesive contagion. Recent simulation studies have cast doubt on the plausibility of the opinion leadership hypothesis, but these simulations are still premised on the favorable assumption that diffusion occurs via contagion.[30] This chapter goes further to suggest that such charitable assumptions may not accurately model some substantive areas, either because diffusion is exogenously imposed or because an endogenous process does not work as a contagion through the network but a spreading miasma over it.

Although the data here are limited to pop songs, the irrelevance of contagion may be an issue for many substantive areas. Exogenous diffusion forces can easily swamp slower-building contagious dynamics, as seen in the contrast between two studies of new drug adoption by physicians—contagion among doctors was strong only with the drug for which the pharmaceutical company refrained from a broad-gauge promotional campaign.[31] States, marketers, and other actors often try to coordinate diffusion and so exogenous patterns may be widely found. Similarly, one can find strong endogenous diffusion when actors are aware of general trends but not those of particular alters.[32] General popularity grows ever more salient with computerized algorithms that arrange the choices facing us by download counts, PageRank, and other measures of popularity.[33] Thus, it may be that not only does opinion leadership require the presence of a preferential-attachment network structure, but also the absence of exogenous forces like promotional campaigns and generalized endogenous structures for information like best-seller lists.

5

THE DIXIE CHICKS RADIO BOYCOTT

In March 2003, the Dixie Chicks were arguably the most popular band in America.[1] Their bluegrass-inflected album *Home* was on the verge of going triple-platinum, their pending American tour for the summer had already sold out most of its dates, and they were number one on both the Country and Adult Contemporary radio airplay charts. This began to change on March 10, 2003, when the Dixie Chicks performed at the London nightclub, Shepherd's Bush Empire. On March 12, the British newspaper *The Guardian* published a brief, three-star review of the concert, approvingly noting that in a "profoundly punk rock" moment, lead singer Natalie Maines told the audience, "Just so you know, we're ashamed the president of the United States is from Texas."[2] On March 14, the Associated Press reported that radio stations had begun dropping the Dixie Chicks from their playlists and engaging in such publicity stunts as providing "trash cans outside the radio station for people to throw their Dixie Chicks CDs away."[3] Maines rapidly apologized for the disrespectful tone of her remarks, but maintained her right to oppose the war, to no avail.

In figure 5.1 I have graphed the total number of times a day the Dixie Chicks were played on American Country radio stations during March 2003. As can be seen, once the story broke, the decline was precipitous.[4] Within a few weeks the Chicks' airplay was a fifth of what it had been before the scandal and they had gone from number one to dropping entirely off the charts. It is clear that the Dixie Chicks were being blacklisted for Maines' contentious statement, but the interesting question is *by whom*?

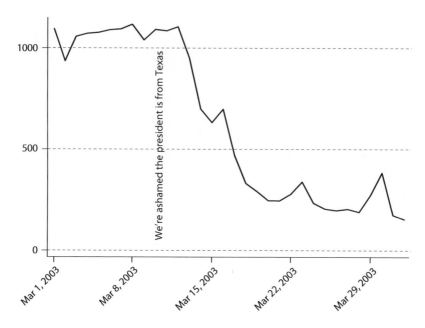

FIGURE 5.1. Daily Spins of Dixie Chicks Songs on Country Stations

5.1 Corporate Censorship

In a March 25, 2003, *New York Times* op-ed, the columnist and econo-mist Paul Krugman accused the massive radio conglomerate Clear Channel of conspiring against the Dixie Chicks and organizing pro-war rallies as a favor to the Bush administration. Part of the alleged motives was that "the Federal Communications Commission is consid-ering further deregulation that would allow Clear Channel to expand even further, particularly into television."[5] Furthermore, Krugman saw personal connections at work, noting that a Clear Channel executive had business dealings with Bush in the 1990s. The notion advocated by Krugman that Clear Channel deliberately punished the Dixie Chicks for their political statement became a small bit of received wisdom in some circles.[6]

Attributing the Dixie Chicks' blacklist to corporate censorship is one piece of evidence offered for a popular vein of criticism of Clear Channel: that the company is enforcing right-wing media hegemony. In fact, in recent years Clear Channel has directed most of its political contributions to the Republican Party, but the allegation goes further to argue that it also biases its *content* to promote right-wing interests. Ben Bagdikian's *New Media Monopoly* provides one particularly blunt version of the argument:

> Daytime radio, dominated by the largest owners, has become
> a right-wing propaganda machine with crudities and right-
> wing consistency that shock and puzzle observers from other
> industrial democracies. As noted earlier, the largest radio
> chain in the country, Clear Channel, has twelve hundred
> stations that dwarf all lesser radio broadcasters, with its
> star talk show, Limbaugh's, followed by a similar menu of
> right-wing commentators specializing in crude diatribes and
> juvenile vocabularies. The remainder is canned syndicated
> music censored of any lyrics that hint of social-conscience
> ideas.[7]

Likewise, the preponderance of right-wing talk shows on AM radio
is sometimes attributed to corporate dominance over the medium,
even though the growth of right-wing talk started years before
deregulation.[8]

Allegations of right-wing bias are not limited to Marxist journalism
professors and progressive think tanks. Similar thoughts were voiced by
radio personality Howard Stern when he announced that his defection
to subscriber-based satellite radio was in part because of frustration
with Clear Channel's alleged retaliation for his recent leftward shift
on several issues.[9] Most directly relevant to this book's emphasis on
music programming is a notorious Clear Channel memo giving stations
a list of 150 songs whose references to bombs, airplanes, or pacifism
the chain felt were best avoided in the immediate aftermath of the 9/11
terrorist attacks.[10] At around the same time, Clear Channel fired KMEL
personality "Davey D." Cook, allegedly for commiting such offenses as
interviewing a pacifist congresswoman.

These critiques of Clear Channel are special cases of the argument
that the "corporate media" serves to legitimate capitalist hegemony.[11]
Political economy theorists assume that cultural organizations derive
their primary interests and political influences from ownership. Political
economists have been very attentive to the large increase in the
concentration of media ownership since World War II. Particularly of
note is the shift of media properties from wealthy families to publicly
traded firms, the latter often called "the corporate media." This shift
is important because Marxist theory argues that such mechanisms as
interlocking directorates and tight interconnection to finance capital
make elites in corporate capitalism especially class-conscious.[12] Indeed,
family-run media firms do behave noticeably differently from corporate
media in such respects as the willingness to run prestige publications at
a loss.[13]

61

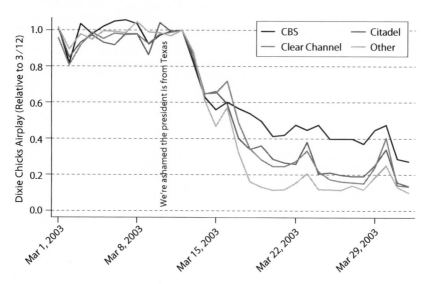

FIGURE 5.2. Daily Spins of Dixie Chicks Songs on Country Stations by Chain

Regulation delayed the general media conglomeration trend for radio until the Telecommunications Act of 1996. Between 1996 and 2000, radio went from extreme ownership dispersion to a fairly concentrated industry, with Clear Channel being by far the largest single firm. As discussed above and in chapter 2, Clear Channel's size and behavior has not made it popular with political economists, activists, recording artists, record labels, or its radio rivals. It was in this context of academic and political discourse about corporate media in general and Clear Channel in particular that Krugman and numerous other commentators accused corporate radio of initiating the Dixie Chicks' blacklisting. However, in chapter 2 we also saw that there is no merit to common allegations that Clear Channel and other radio chains centralize day-to-day programming decision-making, and so it behooves us to listen to the *Porgy and Bess* character Sportin' Life when he tells our heroine that "They tells all you children/The Devil's a villain/But it ain't necessarily so."

Fortunately, the accusation against Clear Channel can be tested with airplay data. In figure 5.2, I have again graphed Dixie Chicks Country radio airplay, but this time broken the data out by corporation.[14] To make the graph easier to read, all lines are set relative to the level of airplay on March 12, the day of the *Guardian* story that indirectly started the boycott. For the first few days of the scandal, the different groups of stations all show similar behavior, cutting Dixie Chicks airplay to about 60 percent of the pre-scandal level. Over the next week they show different rates of decline and thereafter fairly steady levels of airplay.

The interesting thing is that the group of stations that most rapidly and thoroughly abandoned the Dixie Chicks is actually the "other" group. In part this group consists of stations owned by large corporations who simply do not have many Country stations, but it mostly consists of independently owned stations and small regional chains. That is, stations owned by Clear Channel and other large chains like CBS and Citadel did abandon the Dixie Chicks when the band became controversial, however they did so slightly *slower* than did independently owned stations. Hence the large corporations can hardly be said to have instigated the blacklist or to bear special responsibility for it. It seems that station-level programmers at these chains individually responded to the scandal. The only major radio chain to have instituted a corporate-level ban on the Dixie Chicks was Cumulus, which blacklisted the band from all of its Country stations.[15] While stations belonging to the big radio corporations joined in blacklisting the Dixie Chicks, this was not a matter of corporate policy (except at Cumulus) and they did so less aggressively than independently owned stations.

In the counterfactual world where the Telecommunications Act of 1996 never happened and radio chains remained small, the Dixie Chicks would still have been blacklisted, and if anything the blacklisting would have been more rapid and more thorough. This represents a problem for the Marxist political economy perspective. This school is very good at marshaling evidence of both structure (e.g., the corporatization of radio) and hegemonic outcomes (e.g., the Dixie Chicks blacklist), but the causal links between explanans and explanandum are almost always nebulous. Problems like these are why Stuart Hall rhetorically asked:

> Are the "distortions" [of ideology] simply falsehoods? Are they deliberately sponsored falsifications? If so, by whom? Does ideology really function like conscious class propaganda? And if ideology is the product or function of "the structure" rather than of a group of conspirators, how does an economic *structure* generate a guaranteed set of ideological effects? The terms are, clearly, unhelpful as they stand. They make both the masses and capitalists look like judgmental dopes.[16]

5.2 Social Movements

If corporate hegemony does not look like a good explanation for the Dixie Chicks blacklist, we can reasonably ask, what is? A particularly promising suspect is what the political economists Herman and Chomsky (1988) call "flak" from social movements and other aggrieved parties. Social movement organizations actively seek to influence the mass media, and some, such as Media Matters, Media Research Center, the American Family Association, Parents Television Council, Gay and Lesbian Alliance Against Defamation, and Fairness and Accuracy In Reporting, have this as their sole purpose.[17]

The Dixie Chicks situation has parallels to the Hollywood blacklist, which is commonly, but inaccurately, imagined to have been a conspiracy between the studio owners and the House Committee on Un-American Activities (HUAC). In fact, the blacklist is a striking example of the power social movements can exert on the mass media. The 1952 *Miracle* decision put the studios in a very strong legal position from which to face Congress, but competition from television and the 1948 *Paramount* decision ending vertical integration put them in a very weak economic position from which to face a boycott.

Contemporary leftist accounts of the blacklist did not claim that the moguls acted from class interest, personal animus for Communists, or even fear of unfavorable legislation. Rather, the leftist critique of the studios was that they were too "cowardly" to stand up to American Legion pickets.[18] Management and the unions together formed the Motion Picture Industry Council (MPIC) to fight the blacklist, although MPIC eventually adopted a strategy of appeasement. The blacklist and the related "clearance" system were effectively run by the American Legion and other right-wing social movement organizations that published lists of those who had been named by informers or were tied to front organizations. The Legion promised to mobilize their four million members and auxiliaries to picket any film involving these suspected Communists.[19]

One of the things that social movement organizations do is acclimate their members to address a certain set of concerns with a certain repertoire of political tactics. Therefore, a collection of proximately spontaneous acts can meaningfully be considered a form of collective action and part of a social movement.[20] Movements have taught their members that boycotts are an appropriate response to offensive cultural content.[21] This tactic is so practiced that it no longer necessarily requires central coordination.

The statement, "Just so you know, we're ashamed that the president of the United States is from Texas," was indeed taken as offensive by many who heard it. Within hours of the *Guardian* story being published, the "Texas" remark reached American country music fans with a post to the small website, countrynation.com, which had been following the European press coverage of the Dixie Chicks tour. That evening the article was copied in a post entitled "Dixie Chick Tea Party–dump Lipton tea for sponsoring anti-American Chicks!" to the Internet discussion group rec.music.country.western.[22] Concurrently with this, members of the conservative community site Free Republic organized as to boycotting the Dixie Chicks.

On March 13, the day after the *Guardian* article and Internet discussion, the Associated Press published the first story in the major American media on the controversy, noting that "Angry phone calls flooded Nashville radio station WKDF-FM on Thursday, some calling for a boycott of the Texas trio's music."[23] After the wire story, several newspapers carried stories on the subject and Internet discussion abounded, spreading to alt.fan.dixie-chicks and numerous political discussion groups. Much of the Internet discussion referred to the Dixie Chicks as "sluts" and associated them with other anti-war celebrities, as in the insult "hillbilly Jane Fondas." Some posters said they agreed with Maines or discussed the nature of dissent and rebuttals to it in a democracy at war, but many of the posts simply expressed contempt for the musicians. For instance, one post (inaccurately) alleged that fans at the London concert burned an American flag and described the Chicks as "stupid anti-American sluts like Jane Fonda, Barbara Streisand [sic], Jeannie Garafalo [sic], Hillary Clinton, etc."

Just as with the (inaccurate) allegations against Clear Channel, the idea that the Dixie Chick's blacklist was driven by right-wing social movements has empirical implications. If we assume that right-wing activists are most common and/or influential in Republican-leaning areas and that activists are especially likely to petition to local institutions, then the impact of social movement activity should track local politics. In figure 5.3, I disaggregate Dixie Chicks Country radio airplay by the results of the 2000 election for the state within which the station is located. As can be seen, stations in Republican-leaning red states abandoned the Dixie Chicks appreciably faster than did stations in Democrat-leaning blue states.[24]

This trend is entirely consistent with the theory that the Dixie Chick's boycott was fundamentally driven by the political mobilization of right-wing social movements whose members called and wrote to radio stations. The social movement theory of this blacklist also has substantial qualitative evidence behind it, as seen in the documentary film *Shut Up and Sing*. Likewise, in my own correspondence with program directors about the controversy, many of them volunteered unprompted that their decisions were driven by listener demands:

- Once the controversy started, we received numerous calls and e-mails. We decided to pull the song at that time.

65

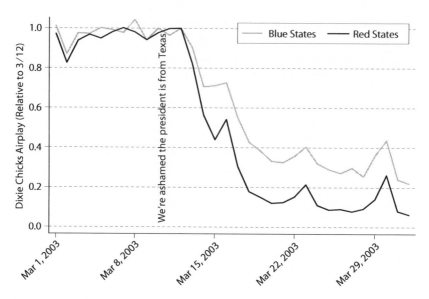

FIGURE 5.3. Daily Spins of Dixie Chicks Songs on Country Stations by 2000 Presidential Vote

- Listener outrage caused us to pull it and that has not changed. Our listeners have been 9-to-1 against [my station] playing the Dixie Chicks. The remarks sure hit a nerve here.
- When The Controversy began, we continued to play Landslide, but within a couple days, we received dozens of e-mails and even more calls from angry listeners. So, what [my station] did was QUIETLY remove the song from our playlist. We made no statements about it, and did not pander to the prevailing jingoism of the majority of our audience. We're a Soft Adult Contemporary music station, and the Chicks don't really fit in all that well anyway. My personal belief is that people in general DO NOT CARE about the political leanings of entertainers. After all, we are just ENTERTAINERS! I doubted the motivations for action in Iraq, too.
- Yes, we were playing them and chose to drop them from our playlist as a result of our own research with our target audience that indicated it had become a polar issue. With our format, we believe that it is more advantageous to not play a record that can hurt you, than to do otherwise. We avoid doing things that will cause our audience to turn the radio off.

One programmer described the "Texas" remark as intrinsically offensive but also mentioned audience feedback. Another invoked station research predating the controversy showing that the audience had tired of the Dixie Chicks (for reasons unrelated to the controversy) and thus his decision to stop playing them was routine and apolitical.[25] However, with these exceptions, programmers described the decision to stop playing the Dixie Chicks as being primarily about acquiescing to the political grievances of listeners. Several of the stations also mentioned their format as interacting with listener demands. As seen in the third quote above, some Adult Contemporary programmers mentioned that as a crossover (from Country) act, the Dixie Chicks were always a tenuous fit with their station even in the best of times. Conversely, some Country programmers said things to the effect that Country audiences reject politically critical remarks.

5.3 Genre

The ideological connotations of country music and the leanings of its audience are worth ruminating on. In the 1920s, a burgeoning commercial recording and broadcasting industry sought out new music beyond New York to feed a ravenous and diverse market.[26] Anthropologists such as Alan Lomax and Tin Pan Alley A&R men such as Ralph Peer recorded "hillbilly" and "race" records, and in the process split a fairly integrated roots music tradition into genres that would eventually become white "country" music and black "blues." In the mid-1920s, Henry Ford sponsored "old timey" musicians, such as Fiddlin' John Carson, as a way to promote a wholesome nationalism grounded in pastoralism and the identity of old white ethnic stocks. In 1953, redhunters in Congress attacked the Communist folk group, The Weavers, splitting the genre further—not by race but by politics.[27] Thenceforth, "folk" music was identified with the political left, whereas "country" music was identified with the political right.[28] By the 1970s, country music had spread from a rural white audience to the urban white working class. Ironically, as country reached a more urban audience, began to use electric instruments, and integrated into the commercial music industry, lyrics "loaded up on signifiers that unambiguously locate the song—and by inference the singer—squarely within the country music tradition."[29] As its various historical names ("hillbilly," "country," "country-western," "folk," and "old timey") imply, country music has always been associated with pastoral white America and its values, such as independence, patriotism, and religion.

Like country music, the related concepts of "Texas" and "cowboy" have strong cultural and political connotations. In the run-up to the

Iraq war, cowboy iconography was frequently invoked to stand for the hawkish position by both proponents and opponents of the war. For instance, several prominent hawks used the 1952 Western film *High Noon* as a metaphor for the war, with the cowardly townsfolk representing the Europeans and the town marshal—who alone has the manly resolve to defend civilization from desperadoes—as the Americans and British. Likewise, opponents of the war also invoked cowboy imagery, with political cartoonists frequently portraying President George W. Bush in a ten gallon hat, Western shirt, jeans, and boots and protesters dressing effigies in similar costume and using variations on the slogan, "Bomb Texas."[30]

Not only were the concepts of "cowboy" and "Texas" thoroughly politicized in early 2003, but so was country music itself. In addition to its long-developing general reputation for conservative politics, country music had taken a gung ho position on both the War on Terror and the Iraq war (with war advocates seeing the latter as a front in the former). Just before the controversy, the Dixie Chicks song "Travelin' Soldier" was sharing the Country chart with Darryl Worley's "Have You Forgotten," which argued that pacifist sentiments were amnesic about the 9/11 terrorist attacks. Even more notable was the Toby Keith song "Courtesy of the Red, White, & Blue (The Angry American)" which reached number one on the Country chart in 2002 and was known for the memorable couplet, "We'll put a boot in your ass, it's the American way." Natalie Maines objected to the themes of the song and publicly feuded with Toby Keith over it. Thus, by the time that Natalie Maines said she was "ashamed that the President of the United States is from Texas," country music as a genre had effectively taken a hawkish position and Maines had already set herself in opposition to this trend.

The fact that the Dixie Chicks had achieved crossover success lets us see the salience of genre by contrasting how quickly they were blacklisted in Country versus less political formats where they were also popular. In figure 5.4, I have graphed airplay for the Dixie Chicks for each of the four formats where they were receiving significant airplay: Country, Adult Contemporary (AC), Top 40, and Hot AC. As seen in the graph, initially the blacklist was almost exclusively a Country phenomenon. After four or five days, the Chicks began slipping in the other three formats as well. The patterns for AC and the various pop formats are essentially identical to each other, contrasting with Country both in being delayed and in being less severe. It is noteworthy in this context that the other formats were (and remain) apolitical, with essentially no songs about foreign policy. Although it is impossible to run the world again and assess the counterfactual, it is possible that the blacklists in these other formats were inspired by the Country blacklist,

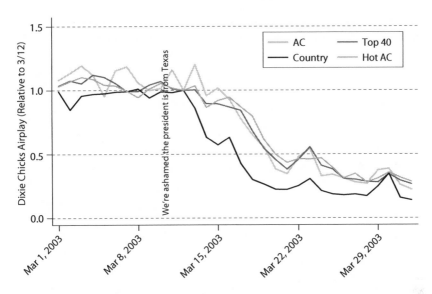

FIGURE 5.4. Daily Spins of Dixie Chicks Songs by Station Format

and thus absent the Country blacklist the Chicks would have remained on other formats as well.

Furthermore, not only did Country format stations reduce the Chicks' airplay more rapidly than did Adult Contemporary and pop stations, but multiple regression analysis shows that conservative local politics have a stronger effect on Country stations.[31] Mathematically stated, Country format not only has a significant negative additive effect on airplay, but also a significant negative interaction effect with measures of conservative public opinion. Thus, it seems that conservative public opinion affects both formats in similar ways, but the ideology of country music magnifies its impact.

Many fans see country music as an oasis of tradition in a world where tradition is besieged by liberal elites. Thus, when country musicians express the same values in the same patronizing tones as those liberal elites, it is not merely disagreeable, but a betrayal of their essential identity. The *Guardian* was right—the "Texas" incident was a punk rock moment; unfortunately for the Dixie Chicks, they are not punk rock musicians with a punk rock audience. Pearl Jam, a punk-influenced rock band, made similar statements without serious consequences.

This analysis has shown no evidence that corporate elites took vengeance against artists who oppose right-wing politics. Boycotts and conflict are a source of instability which business seeks to avoid. The

69

recording and radio industries thrive on star power and have no desire to destroy the viability of any of those relatively few acts who resonate with the public as powerfully as the Dixie Chicks did in March 2003. Rather, the data suggest that country music has a vengeful audience to whose wishes firms responded with varying degrees of haste. Thus, the most important consequence of this analysis is that it turns the Marxist notions of "false consciousness" and "hegemony" on their heads. Rather than corporate interests punishing dissent and imposing right-wing values on the citizenry, in this instance citizens demanded assent to these ideas from corporations. This dynamic was in part structured around genre, a theme to be explored at more length in the next chapter.

6

BUT WHICH CHART DO YOU CLIMB?

The most fundamental issue that defines a radio station is its format. A format is "a package of program content, announcer style, timing of program and commercial material, and methods for obtaining listener feedback and quality control."[1] In other words, format is radio's version of what organizational theory calls a core strategy. Formats structure radio station behavior in every way. Formats determine a demographic and psychographic target audience, as in Chancellor Media's boast to advertisers that it had a "wall of women" of various ages in its Top 40, Dance, 80s Hits, and Adult Contemporary stations in New York.[2] Similarly, most market information is presented by format. Although *Billboard* has a "Hot 100" chart drawing from all formats, but radio programmers find this less useful than the trade's several format-based charts. This is true even for programmers at so-called Top 40 stations, which as discussed below is an anachronistic term.

Format is the primary consideration in programming. Keith Negus tells us that a programmer's "first concern is inevitably whether a particular recording is compatible with the station's format."[3] That is, a program director or music director who is evaluating a song is evaluating it in terms of its relevance for the station's format. Jarl Ahlkvist's ethnographic interviews led him to learn that to programmers "developing an ear for music is important, but the ear that is valued is not one that knows quality music when it hears it, but one that is tuned into what the station's listeners hear in a record."[4] Similarly, in a qualitative interview, a programmer for a Contemporary Christian Music station told me that in his personal time he mostly listens to secular rock stations. Programming is a professional issue, such that "I listen to some songs from the target audience perspective and think, 'would the audience like it?' There are songs I love that have never made it on the radio."

Format so completely structures radio that its effects reach upstream into the music recording industry. Negus describes record company "promotion departments [as being] subdivided into specialists who deal with the different radio formats. In a large number of companies this is rationalized through to the artist development and A&R divisions where different staff or subdivisions deal with different categories of music."[5] This is especially pronounced with the business model developed in the 1960s of record firms having internally autonomous divisions called "labels," which are analogous to imprints in publishing.[6] These labels often specialize by genre. For instance, Universal Music Group contains such labels as Def Jam (hip-hop), Machete (reggaetón), and Island (rock).

This chapter will first provide a qualitative overview of the long-term trend toward increasingly differentiated formats followed by a review of literature on categorical schema in arts and diffusion. I then use "Love Song" to illustrate how diffusion patterns differ when songs cross over to new formats. The chapter closes with a discussion of the emergence of new formats with a case history of how the Hurban format provided a home for reggaetón.

6.1 Trends in the Differentiation of Radio Formats

In light of the powerful ways that radio is structured by formats, it is worth noting that the medium was not always as segmented by genre conventions as it is today. Radio has been experiencing a long-term trend toward increasingly narrowly targeted programming since the 1950s. This is something of a mixed blessing from the perspective of diversity. On the one hand, there are more formats now than in the 1950s, but on the other, any given station today will have much less eclectic airplay than did early stations, which were characterized by a few extremely broad formats. In some sense the long-term trend has been for greater sorting into narrower categories, with the diversity of airplay *within* any given station decreasing, and changes in the aggregate diversity of airplay across the industry being less dramatic than would be suggested by counting types of stations.

From the late 1920s through the early 1950s, the typical radio station played an eclectic mix of programming: news, live or recorded music, sitcoms, dramas, etc. While such "Full Service" programming is now nearly extinct on commercial radio, it set the template for television.

Most of the basic genres of television programming originated in radio, as did the original television networks (i.e., CBS, NBC, and ABC), almost all of television's early stars (e.g., Milton Berle, Jack Benny, Ernie Kovacs), and even entire television programs (e.g., *Guiding Light* and *Amos 'n' Andy*).[7] Television grew rapidly in the 1950s, reaching half of households by 1953.[8] The growth of television tremendously weakened the Full Service radio format as advertisers and talent followed consumers to the new medium and affiliates abandoned the radio networks who had set the standard for Full Service radio programming.[9]

In response to the challenge from television, stations cut costs by relying on the cheapest programming they could find: disk jockeys playing records. This tremendous increase in the space available for content, analogous to what journalism scholars call a "news hole," opened up new possibilities for music programming. The most influential of these innovations was the Top 40 format, invented in 1951 by Todd Storz of KOWH in Omaha after he noticed bar patrons repeatedly choosing the same songs from a jukebox.[10] Concurrently, the invention of the transistor made radios so small and cheap that by the mid-1950s most households owned multiple radios. This had the practical effect that families needn't agree on how to tune the radio, which gave radio stations the incentive to offer more demographically targeted programming.[11] Susan Douglas notes that during the 1950s, "stations also became more specialized, developing distinct personalities and catering to specific market segments by playing 'beautiful music,' airing talk shows, or repeating Top 40 over and over. What would eventually be called narrowcasting began as stations targeted teens, or Christians, or country and western fans, or African Americans with particular music and focused advertisers, all presented by distinctive announcers."[12]

Nonetheless, the development of distinct formats in AM radio only developed so far and Top 40 continued to dominate the band into the mid-1960s. This dominance relaxed only with the commercial development of FM in the 1960s, and especially the FCC's 1965 rule against AM/FM simulcasts, which had the effect of opening up space for new styles of programming (much as had the migration of Full Service to television a decade earlier). In 1967, Tom Donahue of KMPX-FM in San Francisco created a new "Underground" radio format that was primarily focused around cultivating an intense attachment to the late 1960s counterculture and only secondarily with music itself.[13] Further formats developed on the FM band in the late 1960s and throughout the 1970s. Among the most notable of these was wonky consultant Lee Abram's creation "Album-Oriented Rock" (AOR)—what most listeners would now call "Classic Rock" or just plain "Rock." AOR refined the

73

rock focus of Underground and married it to the professionalism and mass sensibility of Top 40. Likewise, both Country and black-oriented stations became increasingly common in this period, with the latter developing into the "Soul" format.

Perhaps most surprising, around 1980, "Top 40" began to lose its literal meaning as a chimera of chart toppers, usually on the AM band, slowly transformed into the more focused "Contemporary Hits Radio" (CHR), usually on the FM band. This change became official in October 1992 when *Billboard* distinguished between the "Hot 100" (its old universal chart) and a new "Top 40 Mainstream" chart (focused on CHR). Dance pop musicians like Madonna dominated the Mainstream chart and tended to rank higher there than they did on the Hot 100. In contrast, when artists like Guns N' Roses, who adhered to genre conventions distant from those of pop, did appear on the Mainstream chart, they tended to do so with songs like "November Rain" that compromised with pop genre conventions. Even then these songs appeared lower on the Mainstream chart than they did on the Hot 100. Thus, beginning around 1980 and culminating in the early 1990s, what was once radio's core format organized around whatever was popular became yet another genre-based format, specifically the pop genre.[14]

By about 1980, radio was thoroughly carved into formats, especially in the FM band. However, it was still common in large markets for several stations to compete head-to-head in the most popular formats, even though greater diversity (and aggregate listenership) could be achieved were one of the stations to adopt a new format for which there was unsated demand. Spatial competition models in economics attribute such market structures to firms over-targeting the median consumer.[15] These game theoretic models suggest that such market failure can be most easily avoided through mergers, since a rational firm will not compete with itself. Ironically the most recent increases in format diversity are therefore most plausibly attributable to oligopolization following deregulation with the Telecommunication Act of 1996.[16]

The finding that deregulation produces format diversity has proved controversial in part because the FCC used this research to support further relaxing regulations against concentrated ownership throughout the George W. Bush administration. A major criticism of the research is that it treats format as an unproblematically meaningful categorical concept and overlooks that many formats (such as "Rhythmic" and "Urban") are extremely similar to one another.[17] Indeed, there is no single agreed-upon categorical schema for radio. Mediabase uses a fine-grained schema that, for instance, distinguishes between "Alternative" and "Active Rock," whereas Nielsen's Broadcast Data Systems and

Billboard magazine collapse these two formats under the umbrella term of "Modern Rock."[18] The BIA/fn database has a similar schema to that used by BDS and *Billboard*, but allows for a station to fall in multiple categories, whereas the other datasets treat formats as mutually exclusive. As it happens, the deregulation effect is robust to format definitions as the finding replicates even with a radically different conception of format based on multidimensional scaling of playlists.[19] However, this debate over how meaningful formats are and where one format ends and another begins serves to highlight how problematic categorical schema can be. Such concerns about how categories structure action has been a burgeoning area in sociology.

6.2 Classification and Art

The implications of how particular things are sorted into overlapping categories is an increasingly important problem in sociology, sitting at the nexus of organizational ecology, neo-institutionalism, the sociology of knowledge, and the sociology of culture. Understanding to what categories a market actor belongs implies a whole host of questions, such as with whom is the actor in competition, what is the actor's reference or peer group for purposes of understanding appropriate behavior, and do potential customers or investors even notice the object, and if so how do they evaluate it?[20]

This is an especially important issue in culture since art is thoroughly saturated by issues of genre.[21] Genre serves to provide a set of common understandings about art, which makes possible collaboration and exchange. DiMaggio's (1987) influential theoretical formulation "Classification in Art" gave many theoretical propositions for how broad social structure and proximate issues of cultural production could shape the nature of "Art Classification Systems" in terms of differentiation, hierarchy, universality, and ritual strength. As described above, radio has experienced a long and persistent trend toward increasing differentiation. However, this raises important issues for its universality (i.e., the extent to which all members of society share the same cognitive map of genres). DiMaggio's proposition C-6 suggests that "The more differentiated the system of genre classification, the less universal."[22] In other words, the more complex a schema is, the harder it is to agree on it. Subsequent empirical work has elaborated the causes and consequences of universality, such that falling into several categories benefits products except insofar as it causes the product to have a fuzzy identity, in which case its reception suffers.[23]

One way we should be able to see actors reacting to categories is through diffusion patterns. As Stan Lieberson shows in *A Matter of Taste* and several related articles, baby names are subject to rapid turnover, to the extent that you can make a reasonable guess at a person's birth cohort entirely from his or her first name. Fashionable names do not come at random, but are clustered by phonemic patterns and etymology.[24] For instance, girls' names with a leading "J" were especially popular in the mid-twentieth century as were, for both genders, names with a biblical etymology in the 1970s and names with an Irish etymology in the 1980s (including Irish surnames and place-names repurposed as first names like "Ryan" and "Shannon"). Currently, anyone who ventures into a university-affiliated daycare center and reads the labels on the cubbies will see an abundance of Victorian names. The phenomenon of particular names being clustered by phoneme or etymology is most pronounced among black girls since the late 1960s, whose names often follow consistent phonemic patterns that are subject to fashion even when the particular names are not infrequently entirely novel.[25]

Thus we tend to see the diffusion of particular innovations, such as the recent popularity of several minor variations of the name "Bella," being shaped by the broader popularity of the category to which they belong, such as the current fad for Victorian baby names. Note that this has implications for the patterns by which later versus earlier innovations within a category will diffuse. If we assume certain scope conditions, most notably immediate universal awareness and availability, then innovations from established categories will spread exogenously, whereas those from novel categories will spread endogenously.[26]

When an actor evaluates an innovation, the actor first considers it in terms of the various criteria in the actor's toolkit. If the innovation is sufficiently meritorious by these criteria, the actor may adopt immediately. Scaled up to the macro level this implies an exogenous diffusion pattern. In contrast, when an innovation seems dubious when measured by the actor's rubrics, the actor will delay adoption until a sufficiently convincing mass of the actor's peers have adopted.[27] If actors are using categories as criteria for evaluation, then we should see actors who thoroughly accept a category adopt by exogenous patterns those innovations that cleanly belong to that category. In contrast, actors who see a category as unfamiliar or liminal to their purview should adopt innovations in that category only endogenously or not at all.

We can see this pattern of familiarity with a category structuring diffusion patterns by contrasting the famous case of hybrid corn with the obscure case of hybrid sorghum.[28] One thing that is often overlooked about hybrid corn is that it represented a radical break with existing agriculture because it does not breed true, meaning that farmers need to buy new seed each planting season rather than saving some of the previous harvest as seed. Not surprisingly, farmers were hesitant to adopt this seed until they saw neighbors use it successfully. However, the patterns for subsequent hybrid crops were more complex. Farmers from temperate areas who were familiar with hybrid corn rapidly adopted hybrid sorghum. Tellingly, hybrid sorghum was not initially popular with farmers from arid areas who had no experience with hybrid corn, even though it was very well-suited for their climate. Similar patterns may be at work in the case of radio. That is, we should see different patterns for songs that clearly belong to a format as compared to those that are crossing over from other formats or whose genre is emerging and has only a tentative claim to inclusion in the format.

6.3 Crossover

Pop songs are typically released initially in one format or a few closely related formats. However, there is only so much airplay and only so many listeners a song can get in a format, so crossing over to additional formats allows a song to grow further. Negus describes the process as "firstly, artists, or specific recordings, are defined in terms of a particular radio format. Relevant stations are then targeted, with the aim of 'crossing over' from one format to another and eventually gaining airplay on CHR and across the various formats."[29] This paradoxically presents the problem that the song was highly focused on the genre conventions of its initial format and by definition will not match additional formats as well. Record labels will go so far as to remix the single to better meet the crossover format's genre conventions, but still it will not usually have new tempo, lyrics, or instruments and so is only a loose fit with the new format.[30] Thus we should expect that songs will fit better with the genre conventions of their first format and, by extension, should have different diffusion patterns for initial as compared to crossover formats.

We can see this illustrated in figure 6.1 with "Love Song" by Sara Bareilles, the third most popular song of 2008. Like all immensely popular songs, "Love Song" reached its position on the basis of airplay in multiple formats. In this case those formats were AAA, Hot AC, Top 40, and Adult Contemporary.[31] "Love Song" is a catchy up-tempo soft rock song by a female singer-songwriter and is an almost perfect example of the kind of music played in the Hot AC format. In May 2007, the song began spreading through Hot AC and AAA by a constant hazard. The song was beginning to approach saturation of these two formats in October when it slowly began to cross over into Top 40. The song is not as good a fit with Top 40, as the format is dominated by

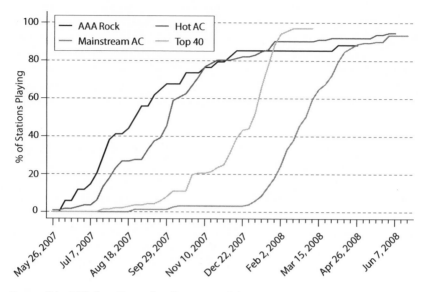

FIGURE 6.1. Diffusion Curve for "Love Song" by Sara Bareilles in AAA, Hot AC, Mainstream AC, and Top 40 Radio

hip-hop and dance music, with soft rock having a sizable but decidedly secondary role in the format. As such, the song spread slowly at first then began to experience exponential growth in November, which continued through December and January until by February the song had saturated the format via a classic s-curve diffusion pattern. The spread to Adult Contemporary tipped even later, in January 2008, with high growth through achieving saturation in April.[32]

Thus we see "Love Song" first spreading by constant hazards, indicating that stations adopted without reference to their peers. Such behavior is theoretically consistent with the stations making the decision to adopt on the basis of their own reading of the song as measured against the genre conventions of the format. Following this we see the song spreading by s-curves through two formats, indicating that the stations were sensitive to peer behavior as their hazard was a function of prior peer adoptions. Note that this endogenous pattern is with regard to their format peers and not stations in adjacent formats. If the adoption of "Love Song" by Top 40 or Adult Contemporary stations were driven by the prior adoptions of "Love Song" by Hot AC stations, these adoptions would have come earlier and the Top 40 and AC curves would look more concave than a classic s-curve. Thus, for songs that are a dubious fit with a station's format, it is insufficient for the song to have been validated by stations in a similar format as the programmer knew ex ante that the song was a better fit with the adjacent format. Rather such a dubious song must be validated by peers in the station's own format.

Most songs do not achieve appreciable success in multiple formats, but among those that do, the single most common pattern is spreading by a constant hazard through a few formats for which it is a close genre fit and then when the song spreads through later formats for which it is a looser fit, it does so by an s-curve.[33] Only in a very few cases does a song's crossover success follow a constant hazard. For instance, the Alicia Keys song "No One" spread exogenously through Rhythmic, Urban, and Urban AC, and then spread by s-curve through Top 40, all of which is consistent with the general pattern. Then two months after its initial success, it began spreading among Hot AC stations through a constant hazard. Similarly, "Move Along" by All-American Rejects spread exogenously through Alternative but only reached a bit more than half of those stations and then, six months later, caught a second wind and spread exogenously through Top 40 until it saturated the format. These cases, however, are atypical compared to songs that either do not experience crossover at all or do so only by s-curves.

Further note that while "Love Song" spread first through soft rock formats before crossing over to Top 40 (and Adult Contemporary), this is not a universal pattern. Top 40 is traditionally understood as a crossover format, and many qualitative descriptions of the crossover process suggest that Top 40 lags the other formats.[34] This was probably the case when the Top 40 format was still an aggregate of hits regardless of genre. However, now that the format has transformed into CHR, with a particular genre focus on pop dance music, it often happens that songs can have their initial popularity in Top 40 and later cross over into other formats. For instance, the Rihanna songs discussed in chapter 2 spread by exogenous patterns through Top 40 concurrently with their spread through the hip-hop formats of Rhythmic and Urban. Similarly, "Pocket Full of Sunshine" by Natasha Bedingfield first spread through Top 40 by a constant hazard (in January through March 2008), then endogenously through Hot AC (March through May) and Mainstream AC (June through August). To the extent that any formats systematically tend to lag behind others, they are not Top 40 but the formats with an older demographic: Adult Hits, Adult Contemporary, and Urban Adult Contemporary.

We have been considering how songs cross over from their first format to subsequent formats but have taken the genre conventions that define formats themselves as stable and unproblematic. Of course, our current genre schema is not an eternal truth of natural law, like the speed of light or the distinctions between elements in the periodic table. Rather, genre conventions are social constructs that are constantly being invented and institutionalized.[35] We can thus watch the diffusion patterns of songs in a new genre change as the genre becomes institutionalized as a legitimate part of a format's programming mix.

6.4   New Genres and Formats

One corollary of crossover diffusion is that it applies to those songs that have a home format. However some songs, and even entire genres of music, don't fit cleanly into *any* formats. For these songs all formats are crossover formats, but without even the validation of performance in the home format. A radio field that is highly structured by format may be particularly inhospitable to music that breaks with extant genre conventions. This is not an issue to the extent that the music industry has only weakly institutionalized categories, but to the extent that the industry is thoroughly segmented by category, it will inhibit the growth of music that breaks with these categories for the same reasons that a securities market that is segmented by industry will penalize conglomerates.[36]

The late 1970s and early 1980s present an interesting case because AM was still largely characterized by the traditional Top 40 format (that is, an eclectic agglomeration of whatever is popular) whereas FM was characterized by narrow formats. As a result, "FM radio, now rigidly segmented by music styles, came late to the disco party. The [FM] dial was sliced into such narrow niches that the new music didn't fit any existing categories and therefore had nowhere to go."[37] Disco presents an extreme case since not only did it fail to conform to the genre expectations of the existing formats, but some stations in existing formats engaged in elaborate boundary work against disco, most notably with the WLUP-FM "disco sucks" rally in July 1979 at the Comiskey Park baseball stadium in Chicago.[38]

Similarly, contrast Bad Religion and the Dropkick Murphys, both of which are punk bands with mostly regional followings (in California and New England, respectively). In 2007, their albums had similar sales but Bad Religion got about twice as much airplay as Dropkick. A good start at an explanation as to why is to consider that Bad Religion's power-pop inflected punk is a much cleaner fit with the genre conventions of the Alternative radio format than is Dropkick's blend of punk and Irish folk music. For instance, Dropkick's lead single in 2007 was "The State of Massachusetts," which prominently features a banjo playing a part that would normally be arranged for an electric guitar and with a tin whistle underscoring the chorus. Such use of folk instruments is odd by the conventions of the Alternative format, and this may explain why radio programmers were skeptical of a fairly popular band—they are just too dubious of a fit with any format. Note that the issue is *not* that the Dropkick Murphys are uniquely bizarre—they are as similar to the Real McKenzies or the Pogues as Bad Religion is to Pennywise or the Pixies—but that they do not fit well with any radio format. For them to garner more regular and extensive airplay would require the emergence of a Celtic rock format or the reconceptualization of an existing format (probably Alternative or Active Rock) to include this subgenre as a regular part of the programming mix.

6.4.1 Reggaetón Comes to the Mainland

Ideally, then, we want to see how songs from a major new genre spread over the course of that genre becoming more institutionalized in radio. While bagpipe punk has never really taken off, there is the case of the even more distinctive new genre of reggaetón. Among the most popular reggaetón artists are Daddy Yankee, Don Omar, Tego Calderon, Wisin y Yandel, and Ivy Queen. Reggaetón is rapped like hip-hop rather than sung like pop or toasted like reggae, and the themes of the lyrics are also similar to hip-hop, although reggaetón is usually in Boricua Spanish or Spanglish rather than African American Vernacular English. The main musical difference between reggaetón and hip-hop is a distinctive fast and tinny staccato dance beat borrowed from Jamaican dancehall music (hence the name "reggaetón").

The mixture of American hip-hop and Jamaican dancehall reflects reggaetón's origins as "Spanish reggae," a cultural cross-pollination between Puerto Rican and Jamaican migrant workers in Panama. The genre continued to evolve as part of Puerto Rican club culture, which to that point had been heavily influenced by hip-hop from the mainland. Although reggaetón traces its origins to a confluence of influences that in 2004 were already very familiar (hip-hop) or somewhat familiar (dancehall) to American radio listeners, the reggaetón sound developed on the island and was jarring when it reached the mainland fully formed. The genre was the musical equivalent to finches blown to an island where they evolve in isolation and by the time their descendants get blown back to the mainland they can no longer interbreed with the ancestral population.

While reggaetón dates back to the 1990s in Panama and Puerto Rico, it did not become popular in the mainland United States until 2004. In that year, Daddy Yankee's album *Barrio Fino* reached number 1 on the *Billboard* Latin chart and number 26 on the general *Billboard* chart. Likewise, reggaetón artists had highly successful concert tours

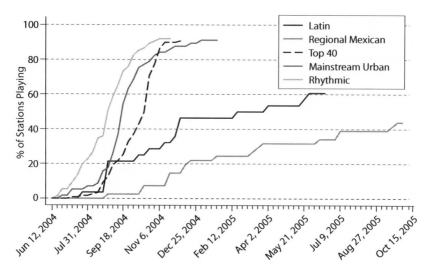

FIGURE 6.2. Diffusion Curve for "Oye Mi Canto" by N.O.R.E., Nina Sky, and Daddy Yankee

of the mainland. Of most direct interest to this chapter, reggaetón artists began getting appreciable radio airplay for the first time in the mainland United States.

The first major reggaetón hit in the mainland United States was "Oye Mi Canto." The song was released in 2004 by N.O.R.E., an English-speaking New York rapper of Puerto Rican descent, but prominently featured the Puerto Rican reggaetón star Daddy Yankee rapping in Spanish. As befits a song primarily credited to a rapper, the song first began spreading in the Rhythmic format, followed closely by Urban and Top 40. However, as seen in figure 6.2, the single followed an s-curve diffusion pattern in these hip-hop and pop formats.[39] In the first 30 days, only 13 stations added the song. Nor were these early adopters arbitrary. Of these 13 adds in the first month of circulation, nine were to stations located in cities with large Puerto Rican populations. In its second month, though, the song not only tipped to experience more rapid adds, but most of these adds were in markets like Phoenix, El Paso, and Los Angeles with hardly any Puerto Ricans but large Mexican populations. Hip-hop and pop stations in markets with few Latinos at all, mostly in the South and Midwest, tended to be late to adopt the song. Thus, we not only see a pattern of slow growth leading up to a tipping point, but also diffusion across a gradient of social distance from reggaetón's Puerto Rican base. All of this is consistent with a pattern of programmers being uncertain about the song's fit and taking cues both from their peers and their audience in attempting to assess the song, rather than just immediately playing the song on or shortly after the add date, as would be typical for a song's first format.

"Oye Mi Canto" not only got airplay on English-language Rhythmic, Urban, and Top 40 stations, but also in Latin radio. Latin radio has several formats, but I collapse all of them together (except for Mexican Regional) as they overlap heavily and the stations are few in number, making aggregation necessary to achieve reasonable sample size. As seen in figure 6.2, the (non-Mexican Regional) Latin formats were even slower than the English-language hip-hop and pop formats to play "Oye Mi Canto." Early on, only one Latin station played the song and then concurrently with it tipping in the English-language formats in late August, it also got several adds in the Latin formats with continuing slow growth through the fall that only reached less than two-thirds of these stations. The song also got some airplay on Mexican Regional stations, but this airplay was last of all. Thus, ambivalent as the English-language formats were about "Oye Mi Canto," the Latin stations were even more so. In order for reggaetón to grow, it would need for some radio formats to take on the music as a regular part of the programming mix.

6.4.2   The Development of the "Hurban" Format as an Artistic and Market Niche

Figure 6.3 shows the the growth of radio airplay for reggaetón during 2004 and 2005. This figure summarizes airplay data for stations who played hip hop or Latin (other than Mexican Regional) and can be interpreted as the probability for any given week of tuning in to a radio station of the appropriate format and (conditional on not getting an advertisement or other non-music content) hearing reggaetón. Because Latin radio experienced large amounts of format flipping during this period, I first used quarterly BIA/fn reports to identify stations with the format of "Spanish" and then compared the stations' actual airplay week by week to the monthly charts for Spanish Tropical, Spanish CHR, and (eventually) Spanish Urban, with stations entering the sample when their airplay approximates these charts.[40] Although relatively few stations flipped in or out of Urban and Rhythmic during this period, for consistency I used the same procedure to create the sample of hip-hop formatted stations. I then coded the sample's airplay by coding a song as being reggaetón if either the main or featured performer is described as a reggaetón artist in the *All Music Guide*. As already seen with the example of "Oye Mi Canto," this practice of a reggaetón artist collaborating with an established hip-hop or pop performer was common early in the popularization of the genre. Finally, because the

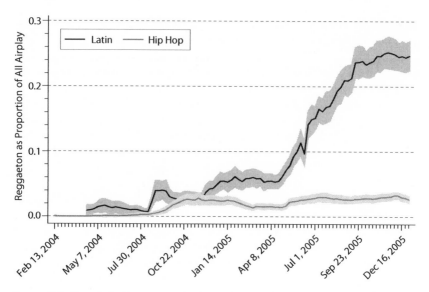

FIGURE 6.3. Growth in Reggaetón Airplay (with Bootstrapped Confidence Intervals), 2004–2005
Note: Latin includes Spanish CHR, Tropical, and Hurban but not Mexican Regional

success of pop songs follows a power-law distribution, it would be easy to mistake a particular fluke hit from a reggaetón artist for a general trend regarding reggaetón as a genre. To avoid a naive reading of the reggaetón trend line, I used bootstrapping to create confidence intervals. The confidence intervals grow wide when reggaetón's airplay is a function of a few huge hits and narrow when the genre's popularity is based on many moderately popular songs.

Throughout this period, reggaetón gets some airplay on hip-hop (i.e., Rhythmic and Urban) radio stations but never accounted for more than 3 or 4 percent of airplay. Furthermore, the lower bound of the confidence interval for the hip-hop radio trend line seldom goes above 2 percent of airplay, suggesting that what airplay reggaetón did achieve on hip-hop stations was always an issue of a few singles achieving crossover success. Thus, at most we can say that reggaetón was a frequent guest within hip-hop, but never at home. However, in Latin formats other than Mexican Regional, reggaetón seems to have become institutionalized as a substantial and regular part of the programming mix. The airplay of reggaetón in Latin radio rises as an s-curve, with a slow build throughout 2004 and then a tipping point in May 2005 that launches rapid growth in the genre's popularity, before plateauing in October 2005 at about a quarter of (non-Mexican Regional) Latin airplay.[41] Furthermore, the confidence intervals show us that this success is attributable to the genre as a whole, and not just a few hits that happen to belong to it.

In understanding how reggaetón grew in Latin airplay, we can consider KXOL-FM in Los Angeles, where I personally heard reggaetón for the first time. In June 2005, the station abandoned its old format of Spanish Adult Contemporary, playing artists like Julieta Venegas and Franco De Vita, and rebranded itself as "Latino 96, Hip Hop y Reggaetón." It immediately (but briefly) became the number two Los Angeles station overall and number one among teens and young adults.[42] KXOL is typical of how reggaetón went beyond the early adopters and tipped to a mass phenomena. First, note that the timing is right—June 2005 is shortly after reggaetón's share of (non-Mexican Regional) Latin airplay tipped around mid-April 2005. Second, notice the demographics of Los Angeles. Less than 1 percent of the Greater Los Angeles population is Puerto Rican or other Spanish Caribbean origin. However, a third of Los Angeles is Mexican origin and almost another 10 percent from other Latin origins (mostly Central Americans). Thus, for reggaetón to succeed in Los Angeles, it could not limit its appeal to the nearly non-existent local Puerto Rican population but had to attract other audiences, especially other Latinos.

Such a large and growing population as Latinos is immensely attractive to cultural firms and advertisers, but only when aggregated into a single Latino population rather than a series of national-origin groups. Over the course of the 1970s and 1980s these commercial interests, in conjunction with the Census Bureau and activists seeking a more effective political coalition, created "Latino" or "Hispanic" as a commercial, demographic, and political category.[43] Although the national-origin groups aggregated into the category were racially and culturally diverse, it was mostly defined by a shared heritage of the Spanish language. Of course "Spanish" itself is something of a misnomer as, like most languages, Spanish consists of many dialects that are mutually intelligible but can serve as regional shibboleths. Early attempts to create Spanish-language broadcasting got hung up on reluctance of Puerto Rican audiences to watch the Mexican-oriented programming on Univision and the reluctance of Mexicans to watch the (initially) Puerto Rican-oriented programming on Telemundo.[44] Thus, the development of a pan-Latin media market required the development both of a "neutral" or "generic" Spanish dialect and more broadly of a generic "Latino" culture built as much around the new pan-ethnic media itself as the relatively weak primordial cultural affinities of such a diverse population.[45]

The main unifying force of pan-Latino popular culture is the Spanish language, and not surprisingly, Spanish-language broadcasters and marketers emphasize the number of Latinos who know the language.[46] It is in this light that it is important to note that 60 percent of American Latinos were born in the United States. This is significant because the vast majority of Latinos who are native born (or who migrated before the age of ten) speak fluent English.[47] In general, a *majority* of Latinos have no language barrier (and a readily bridgeable social distance) to mainstream anglophone culture, but may *also* have a more or less fluent command of Spanish and more or less strong sense of themselves as an ethnic community.

This is an important distinction from the perspective of targeting Latinos as a media audience, since the traditional strategy of providing Spanish-language content to Spanish speakers is less obviously relevant to people who primarily speak English. Spanish-language broadcasters face the uncomfortable fact (which they do their best to obfuscate) that Latinos spend a large majority of their viewing with English-language broadcasts.[48] Indeed, as a Latin television executive confessed, "The principal menace which faces the Latino market in North America, in the long term, is assimilation. Today, you have mom and dad who watch telenovelas and listen to Latin music, and you have the kids who watch an American TV show in their bedroom and listen to hip-hop."[49] Various media ventures launched since the late 1980s and early 1990s use English-language content to appeal to younger English-dominant Latinos. For these English-dominant Latinos and the media that are meant to appeal to them, Spanish can be less a viable means of communicating ideas than a mechanism for signaling identity. The second biggest Hispanic magazine in America (after *People en Español*) is *Latina*, a publication comparable to *Cosmo* which is mostly in English but code-switches the occasional word into Spanish.[50] Similarly, as seen in figure 6.4, the English-language cable channel Sí TV (now called nuvoTV) describes its audience to advertisers as drawn from a demographic who "speak English" but "live Latin," and who not incidentally represent 60 percent of Latino buying power and are "tech-savvy early adopters." Similarly, a more recent ad describes the audience as "American's bi-cultural Latinos."

Reggaetón as an American phenomenon is an extension of the media logic of providing content that appeals to thoroughly acculturated English-dominant Latinos. A telling remark comes from a programmer who explained the success of reggaetón to *Billboard* on the logic that "[f]or many years, the Hispanic community has settled for Rhythmic, Top 40, and hip-hop stations. Finally, there are radio stations that reflect their culture and musical tastes, which is a win-win for everyone."[51] In one sense, this is absurd with regard to, for instance, the two-thirds of American Latinos who are of Mexican origin. Insofar

FIGURE 6.4. Trade Advertisements for the Sí TV/nuvo TV Cable Channel. Courtesy of nuvoTV

as young Mexican Americans' "culture and musical tastes" are those of any other American youth, they do take hip-hop as their music. On the other hand, insofar as Mexican Americans' "culture and musical taste" is directly related to their ethnic origins, this might involve music like banda, norteño, or even narcocorridos rather than reggaetón. For a Mexican American to listen to reggaetón is no more a reflection of her traditions than for an Irish American to embrace polka or a Persian American to pick up klezmer. And yet reggaetón undeniably did resonate with young Latinos, regardless of national origin, and this is an indication of the extent to which "Latino" has become a meaningful identity such that Latinos from one national origin would see pop culture developed by Latinos of a different national origin as *their* cultural accomplishment: something that particularly resonates with them and in which they can take pride of ethnic ownership. Since 2004, reggaetón musicians have deliberately crafted an appeal to English-dominant Latinos of various national origins. The very first American reggaetón hit, "Oye Mi Canto," had lyrics in English and Spanish and contains numerous appeals to Latino identity cross-cutting race or national origin, most notably with a chorus consisting of a list of Latin nationalities and races sung (in Spanish) by the New York pop duo Nina Sky and a video featuring flags and bikini-clad girls representing the various nations of Latin America. Similarly, in 2004, Daddy Yankee began collaborating with anglophone mainland rappers and learned English, a language in which he not only gives interviews but occasionally raps.[52]

Radio has attempted to leverage reggaetón to appeal to English-dominant Latinos through the Hispanic Urban (or "Hurban") format. Hurban stations typically spend about half of their airtime playing reggaetón, a quarter with Spanish-language hip-hop, and a quarter with English-language hip-hop. The word "Hurban" is internal radio jargon and the stations typically advertise themselves as being "Hip Hop y Reggaetón" or "Latino." Since the radio format is meant to appeal to English-dominant Latinos, the disk jockeys usually speak on the air in English, occasionally code-switching to Spanish for rhetorical effect. The format was developed by WVOZ-FM in Puerto Rico, but embraced by Univision, Spanish Broadcasting Systems, Infinity, and Clear Channel, all of whom flipped existing mainland stations to the format.[53] If we return to figure 6.3, we can see that reggaetón's share of Latin radio (other than Mexican Regional) tipped in the spring and summer of 2005. This was in part an issue of Spanish CHR and Tropical stations that had been playing reggaetón for years increasing the frequency with which they did so, but also an issue of stations flipping from completely different formats to the new Hurban format, with reggaetón at the core of their playlists.

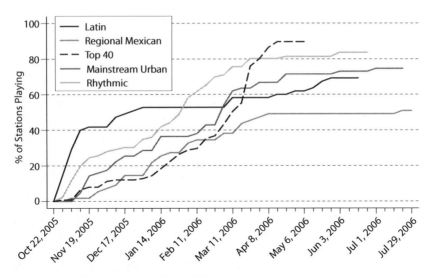

FIGURE 6.5. Diffusion Curve for "Rompe" by Daddy Yankee on Latin and Hip-Hop Radio

Figure 6.5 shows the diffusion of the song "Rompe" by Daddy Yankee, which was released in October 2005, toward the tail end of reggaetón's mainstream success. As seen in figure 6.3, by late 2005, reggaetón formed a regular part of Latin programming, and indeed formed the core of the new Latin format Hurban. During this later period, new reggaetón songs should show rapid diffusion in Latin radio typical of songs spreading in a format that embraces their genre conventions but still be treated as a crossover phenomenon in Urban, Rhythmic, and Top 40. In figure 6.5, "Rompe" spreads rapidly through (non-Mexican Regional) Latin stations by a constant hazard function. Just as important, by this time there were more of these stations.[54] This is the diffusion pattern consistent with a song's home format and what we would expect given the growth of Hurban and reggaetón's popularity more broadly. The pattern for Rhythmic and Urban formats is more mixed. In these formats, "Rompe" experienced a growth curve that reflects a mix of direct influences and endogenous growth. That is, programmers in the hip-hop formats seem to have partially accepted reggaetón (at least in the person of Daddy Yankee) but for the most part they still understood it as a crossover issue, requiring peer validation. Finally, programmers in Top 40 and Regional Mexican both had completely typical adoption patterns for crossover formats. Thus, the spread of this later reggaetón song was exogenous within its main format and essentially endogenous within its crossover format. The format itself, though, grew through a largely endogenous pattern. As the format grew, there were more stations with which reggaetón songs had a good fit and through which they could experience exogenous growth.

More broadly, we can recognize that categories structure behavior, including diffusion behavior. As categories become more established, particular things that are members of those categories may become accepted not only more rapidly, but by a qualitatively different process emphasizing conformity to the category's conventions rather than peer adoption of the particular thing.[55] It is in this sense that the popularity of categories and actors aligning themselves with categories, as in the example of radio stations adopting formats and formats developing to include new genres, becomes important, for it changes how future objects will be received. Although the end result of the institutionalization of categories and alignment of actors with these categories is that innovations can spread exogenously through them, the process of category institutionalization itself involves uncertainty that is ameliorated by the observations and imitations of peers. Thus, while the ordinary processes of radio and other fields can be so routine that actors coordinate without communication, the process of developing those routines is itself a process of entrepreneurial discovery and peer imitation.

7

THE FUTURE OF THE CHART

There is an obvious irony to writing a book in the early twenty-first century on such a consummately twentieth-century medium as radio. Radio as we know it began with the November 1920 launch of KDKA in Pittsburgh. Thus began the transformation of radio from a military and maritime point-to-point communication technology controlled by the Navy into a civilian broadcasting medium. Hundreds of stations went on the air in 1922—the same year that WEAF of New York started selling advertising time.[1] Radio set manufacturers encouraged sales by promoting broadcasting. Most notably, RCA, GE, and Westinghouse cooperated to create the National Broadcasting Company (NBC) network in 1925. As the manufacturers anticipated, the popularity of radio receivers followed the broadcasting signals. From a baseline of almost no receivers in 1922, one in ten households owned a radio in 1925, and one in four by 1927. Growth continued throughout the 1930s and reached about nine in ten homes by the late 1930s and early 1940s.[2] Radio broadcasting was understood as a pinnacle of modernity, both popularly and by the mass society theorists of the time. Max Horkheimer and Theodor Adorno had a particularly dark version of this view in writing that radio was to Nazism as the printing press was to the Reformation.[3] The 1950s saw the introduction of both television and cheap transistor radios, which had the effect of transforming the radio from a medium attentively listened to in the living room to an omnipresent background track everywhere else. These changes allowed increasing diversity, which both promoted the development of intense fan identities and undermined the earlier "mass society" thesis.[4] Although eclipsed by television in cultural significance, radio listening was stable and even increased throughout the 1970s and 1980s.[5]

However, since about 1990, the amount of time the average American spends listening to the radio has been in a steady decline, at a rate of about 1.5 percent per year in the early 1990s and accelerating to about 2 percent a year from 1995 to the present.[6] The decline describes all demographic groups, but is especially pronounced among male listeners aged 12–17 and 18–24. Likewise, industry revenues have been declining (in constant 2002 dollars) from $15.6 billion in 2000 to $13.6 billion in 2007.[7] Plausible theories for explaining this recent decline include the widespread popularity of competing technologies over the period (especially automobile and handheld CD players and MP3 players). Furthermore, the accelerating decline since the mid-1990s suggests possible effects of deregulation, following which many radio conglomerates emphasized cutting costs over increasing listenership.[8]

Of course even if it continues to decline, radio will remain an important medium well into the new century. The general tendency for media that would seem to have been superseded by some new technological marvel is not to disappear entirely, but to retain diminished but sizable audiences for decades.[9] Even if we think it likely that radio will be evicted from its current technological niche in the AM and FM bands by some combination of politics, technology, and economics, we will continue to have some kind of curated audio experience that feels like (and is probably called) "radio."[10] In such a worst case scenario for the stability of radio, the user experience would migrate from traditional terrestrial radio bands to some other technical channel: podcasts, streaming Internet radio, satellite radio, or some as yet unimagined protocol for delivering recorded or live audio programming to users. Nonetheless, even if we can reasonably expect some form of radio to remain with us, it is worth recognizing that the medium's cultural impact is likely to continue to decline in at least relative terms, if not also in absolute terms. In thinking about the future of popular culture, we thus have to think not only about radio but about those media that will in part replace and displace it.

The record industry has already found alternatives to radio in marketing music. Surprisingly, one of the most important of these alternative promotional media is television. Consider the top selling record of 2006, *High School Musical*. With the exception of the tween-oriented "Radio Disney" network, the songs from this album got essentially no airplay on the radio, just a couple dozen spins for all of 2006. Rather, *HSM* attained its success by being the soundtrack to a made-for-cable movie. In addition to the best-selling CD and DVD, Disney has created numerous profitable derived works from the film: a cable sequel, a theatrically released sequel, a reality television show, live stage shows, theme park attractions, and innumerable varieties of branded clothing and merchandise. Likewise, the titan of the spring television schedule is the program *American Idol*, which has a reasonable track record for launching the careers of its winners and finalists.[11] Just as important, *Idol* reinvigorates the sales of the weekly guest coaches, which is why A-list recording artists like Gwen Stefani, Elton John, and Mariah Carey have each devoted a week to coaching what is, in essence, a protracted karaoke contest. The most recent case of Broadway-style music prevailing through the small screen is *Glee*. This is not only an hour-long television show depicting a high school choral club, but a reliable powerhouse of the iTunes download market that places about three songs per episode (all of them choral arrangements of older hits) on the *Billboard* Hot 100 chart. By the middle of its second season, *Glee* had cumulatively placed 113 singles on the chart, breaking the previous record of 108 charting singles for Elvis Presley.[12] The power of television to sell music extends even to commercials for other consumer goods. Since the mid-1990s, musicians have come to see commercial licensing less as "selling out" than as another means of exposure. The licensing of both current and classic songs is now so common and accepted that *Advertising Age* found the real man-bites-dog story to be that some advertisers still commission original jingles.[13] Ironically the most notable exception to television's pop music integration is the moribund music video television format, which MTV and VH1 have gradually abandoned since the late 1990s in favor of reality and magazine programming.

Of course, much more dramatic changes in the music industry came from the Internet. Internet file-sharing has precursors with Internet Relay Chat and alt.binaries newsgroups, but broke into the mainstream in 1999 with the relatively user-friendly Napster service. The previous year saw several early MP3 players, each holding about an hour of audio, and over the next couple of years the market matured with the Creative Labs Nomad Jukebox and the first Apple iPod, each of which held about 70 hours of audio. MP3 players proved to be complements with file-sharing as they allowed one to listen to downloaded music without the intermediate step of burning a CD. Likewise, broadband Internet access (which allows one to download an MP3 in seconds, rather than minutes as with dial-up) was rare at the time but growing rapidly. Though the music industry successfully sued Napster, the music and film industries' larger war against file-sharing has proven to be like a game of whack-a-mole, as Napster was replaced by more truly decentralized architectures which were exponentially more difficult for the music industry to shut down.[14] Under threat from file-sharing, the music industry reluctantly agreed to cooperate with licensed digital music services, most notably iTunes in 2003 and Amazon in 2008, which they had previously resisted as they understood that this would mean selling one or two singles from an album for 99 cents each instead of an entire CD for $14.99. This is only the most recent instance of a recurring pattern in pop culture industries such that, when threatened by pirates, the industry first attempts to suppress piracy and then "assimilates" it by adopting a business model closer to that of the pirated editions, including not only a lower price point but often format innovations introduced by the pirates.[15] Nonetheless, while this legal market for digital downloads has grown rapidly, it has not grown nearly rapidly enough to replace diminished CD sales.[16]

Similarly, a variety of streaming media services have become important to pop music. The video site YouTube hosts large numbers of music videos, both the professionally produced sort that we (somewhat anachronistically) associate with MTV and crude videos created by fans, which can range from cellphone camera footage of live performances to simple album art slide shows with the MP3 as a background track. Some of these videos can be immensely popular. For instance, the Rihanna song "Umbrella" (discussed at length in chapter 2) has two popular copies on YouTube, with a combined 62 million views. Initially major cultural producers (especially Viacom) attempted to suppress piracy of their content on YouTube, but more recently they have adopted an assimilation strategy with the sites Vevo and MTV.com, both of which license music videos from record labels for a share of advertising revenues. As *Billboard* noted, this has the implication that "music videos have gone from a marketing and promotional expense for record labels to the linchpin of their strategy to profit from online advertising."[17] Likewise, audio- only streaming services like Live365, Pandora, and Stitcher allow a smartphone to behave like a radio receiver that receives content over 3G rather than AM or FM.

The music industry is in a period of transformation. The last ten years have seen disruptive innovation challenge the established business model of using broadcasting to promote the sale of recorded music, just as a few generations ago AM radio and vinyl 78 RPM records themselves disrupted the business model of using live performances to promote the sale of sheet music. Thus, a direct reading of the near past is unlikely to prove a reliable guide to the future. Rather, the best way to make predictions is to understand not the past, but the processes that underlie it and then extrapolate how these processes will intersect with changing circumstances. This was the approach taken by Neuman (1991), who was able to accurately map out the broad contours of what the media would look like after it had been transformed by ubiquitous digital technology—even though he was writing at a time when the Internet was still entirely text-based and dial-up modems transferred data at three orders of magnitude below today's broadband speeds. Of course, the early 1990s had no shortage of techno-utopians who understood that Moore's Law was about to make content creation and dissemination so cheap as to be essentially free. What was distinct about Neuman's prediction was that he also understood the social implications of the inherent scarcity of attention, and so he not only predicted blogs, but also that the vast majority of blogs would go unread and the incumbent mass media would retain the bulk of the audience.[18] Similarly, by reviewing how songs currently spread through pop music radio and understanding how radio differs from new and emerging media, we can extrapolate the future of pop music while avoiding excesses of either dystopianism or utopianism. A first step toward such a task is reviewing what we have learned about how pop songs become popular, and how diffusion works more broadly.

7.1 General Lessons of the Book for Diffusion of Innovations

Before getting into the actual findings of the book for how diffusion works in pop music radio, it is worth ruminating on the overall approach: *who* adopts an innovation is less interesting than *how* the innovation gets adopted. It is one thing to show what kinds of farmers are particularly quick to plant a new kind of seed, what kinds of physicians are particularly quick to prescribe a new antibiotic, or what kinds of radio stations are particularly quick to add a new pop single. It is another thing, and I would argue a more fundamental thing, to show what kinds of objects diffuse through populations by which mechanisms. Misunderstanding the mechanism at the innovation level can lead to problems with analyses at the actor level. Much ink has been spilled trying to show which doctors learned about tetracycline from which other doctors because analysts focused on data about relationships between doctors.[19] Sociology's wild goose chase through the medical advice networks of small-town Illinois might have been avoided had we taken more seriously from the get-go the diffusion curve's indication that word-of-mouth between these doctors was dwarfed by something outside of the local medical community, most likely Pfizer's marketing efforts.

Contagion through a social network is just one of several ways that an innovation might spread through a social system. Diffusion can also occur through external influence (e.g., payola), simple field-level endogenous diffusion (e.g., best-seller lists), or field-level endogenous diffusion mediated by network-derived measures of status (e.g., Google's PageRank algorithm).[20] Of course it might also occur by contagion through social networks, especially as traditional forms of contagion (e.g., your friend tells you about her favorite new song) are augmented by performative social network technologies (e.g., your friend microblogs her favorite new song). The point is that contagion is just one of many possible means by which something can diffuse and we might expect contingencies of either the innovation itself or the environment within which it is embedded to affect which of these diffusion mechanisms are at play. And yet most research emphasizes questions of who adopts an innovation first, whether the analysis be about location in the network (e.g., cohesion, structural equivalence) or a methodologically individualistic emphasis on traits (e.g., income, various aspects of personality).

This emphasis on "who does it first" is found in extreme form with semiparametric survival models, especially the extremely popular Cox proportional hazards model. As Cleves, Gould, and Gutierrez (2004) summarize it, "the nice thing about this model is that $h_0(t)$, the baseline hazard, is given no particular parameterization and, in fact, is left unestimated. The model makes no assumptions about the shape of the hazard over time—it could be constant, increasing, decreasing, increasing and then decreasing, decreasing and then increasing, or anything else you can imagine." This of course contrasts with the approach taken in this book, which at a technical level is all about seeing if hazards are constant or increasing. Cleves and colleagues continue by explaining that the Cox model works by "confining our analyses to only those times for which failure occurs and by conditioning on the fact that failures occurred only at those times, the baseline hazard drops out from the calculation."[21] In ordinary English this means that if we know that something happened to somebody at a particular time, we can focus entirely on the question of *to whom* did it occur and ignore the issue of why did it happen *then*. This is a very convenient property insofar as one is interested exclusively in how the traits or network locations of actors will affect their relative haste to adopt, but it leaves aside the innovation's basic pattern of diffusion itself. For instance, application of the Cox model to both hybrid corn and tetracycline might reveal that in both cases cosmopolitanism predicts relatively early adoption. However, the model's very robustness allows (indeed, tacitly encourages) the researcher to ignore the fact that hybrid corn spread endogenously whereas tetracycline spread exogenously.

The problems with emphasizing relative risk to the exclusion of the baseline hazard can be illustrated by returning to diffusion's choleric roots and considering health pathologies. Different types of diseases spread by different mechanisms and any public health researcher worth her (carefully limited daily allowance of) salt will want to know which of these mechanisms is at work for which problems. HIV requires the exchange of bodily fluids like blood or semen and does not persist in the environment, so it follows the network contagion model fairly well, specifically through sex and intravenous drug networks. In contrast, influenzas can be conveyed through the much less intimate act of sneezing and are fairly persistent in the environment, so their diffusion more reasonably approximates a generalized endogenous diffusion process. Finally, onset of radiation sickness from an atomic bomb or nuclear meltdown would follow an external pattern since the radiation is emanating from a central source rather than using hosts to multiply itself as would a virus or bacteria. An approach that brackets the baseline hazard and goes directly to asking "who gets sick first?" is in some sense missing the point. One can certainly find individual-level correlates using such methods, for instance one wouldn't want to be frequenting busy train stations or airports during an influenza outbreak, and it's not a great idea to receive unprotected anal sex during an HIV epidemic. However, in both a theoretical sense and in terms of crafting a public health response, these individual-level correlates are secondary to knowing whether the health problem is an infectious disease transmitted through intimate contact, an infectious disease transmitted through casual contact, or an environmental contaminant.[22]

Both the relative haste of actors and the diffusion mechanism are legitimate research questions, but a major aim of this book is to remind us that the latter is as interesting as the former, and in some ways more fundamental. Fortunately, there are several signs that researchers are beginning to pay more attention to comparing diffusion mechanisms and identifying contingencies for them. The decades-old state policy diffusion tradition in political science has recently begun emphasizing innovations (policies) rather than actors (states) by comparing policies, and noting patterns such as that political no-brainer policies tend to spread by external-influence curves in contrast to s-curves for less obviously popular policies.[23] Linguistics has a well-developed literature on the diffusion of vocabulary and pronunciation that not only addresses questions of who will imitate whom, but also such issues as what sorts of linguistic features diffuse most readily and by what mechanisms.[24] In sociology, recent theoretical developments exemplified by Hedström and Bearman's *Oxford Handbook of Analytical Sociology* (2009) give greater emphasis to mechanism as a theoretical tool, with particular attention to such questions as the various ways change might be exogenous or endogenous to a system.

At a methodological level, advances in computing power have made it easier both to collect and to analyze data in ways that make possible new types of analyses. Traditionally, economic sociology can be described as people who like copying old phone books into Excel. When data collection is this labor-intensive, it doesn't scale very well and not surprisingly analysts tend to emphasize how actors differ in their adoption timing with regard to a single innovation. However Internet-based data collection allows one to much more readily collect vast quantities of data. For instance, computer scientists, physicists, and the occasional sociologist have collected data on thousands of YouTube videos, catch phrases in political discourse, or Twitter posts and then conducted diffusion analyses of these cultural objects.[25]

Thanks to cheap computing power, such torrents of data cannot only be collected but also analyzed in either a meta-analysis or multilevel framework to identify what kinds of innovations (and social contexts) spread by what types of diffusion patterns.[26] This change in the quantity of data, unit of analysis, and analytical strategy implies research questions that are qualitatively different from those one might ask about how a single business practice spread through the *Fortune* 500, and in particular they make it more feasible to ask questions about differences between innovations rather than just the actors who adopt them. For instance, the word "meme" is usually nothing more than a synonym for "innovation" used by people with a background in STEM fields or Internet culture rather than sociology or communications. However, in its original form the concept was used to articulate a hypothesis that ideas which encourage their believers toward evangelism or fecundity will spread more rapidly than other ideas.[27] This is inherently a hypothesis about different kinds of innovations that cannot be seriously investigated by looking at one innovation at a time, but rather only by looking at many innovations and comparing by what patterns and rates they spread. Similarly, we might ask about such issues as conventional marketing, viral marketing, direct cost, opportunity cost, extant competing innovations, anticipation of forthcoming competing innovations, intrinsic utility versus reliance on network externalities, comprehensibility, salaciousness, compatibility with existing culture and infrastructure, etc., and how these affect the ways in which innovations diffuse. By changing the unit of analysis from the actor to the innovation, we open a new set of theoretical possibilities.

7.1.1 Particular Lessons for Diffusion in Pop Music Radio

In the particular case of pop music radio, this book has applied the model of focusing on innovations rather than only actors by asking questions about kinds of songs in addition to questions about kinds of stations. This approach provides a portrait of how the pop music industry experiences the distributor-surrogate boundary point, an issue that the production of culture tradition argues to be the single most important for understanding cultural industries.[28] These findings both dispel some common expectations (centralized coordination within radio chains, diffusion through social networks) and have more positive findings (coordination by labels, the importance of genre conventions, the flow of information at the fieldlevel).

In chapter 1 we saw a brief introduction to the logics of diffusion of innovation and production of culture. Pop music primarily works through a sequential gatekeeping process, with the key boundary point in much of the literature being between cultural distributors who provide infrastructure for the development and distribution of artists (e.g., record labels) and surrogate consumers who publicize artists (e.g., radio stations). In the diffusion of innovation one measures the rate at which an innovation spreads through a social system to estimate whether the innovation seems to be spread by an endogenous dynamic like word of mouth (as reflected in an s-curve) or by an exogenous force like advertising (as reflected in a concave curve).

In the second chapter we saw that pop songs generally follow a pattern consistent with centralized coordination, which raises the question of who or what is coordinating the stations. It cannot simply be the availability of songs, because albums that produce multiple singles find the second and third singles becoming suddenly popular well after stations have access to the songs. Nor can it be coordination at the chain level since radio stations belonging to different chains all add at approximately the same time and essentially no variance in timing is clustered within chain. Nonetheless, this leaves the question of who is coordinating radio, and chapter 3 suggests that the issue is record label promotion efforts, as found in extreme form with payola. Documented instances of payola show especially pronounced concave curves and the concavity of diffusion curves (briefly) declines during periods of higher regulatory scrutiny. The chapter reviews the long history of payola in the music industry and uses game theory to explain why, despite repeated government and industry efforts to stop payola, the practice keeps coming back roughly every 14 or 15 years.

Chapter 4 tackles the idea that some key stations can "break" singles, which is just radio's version of the opinion leadership hypothesis that especially central actors in a social system are key to determining diffusion. To do this the chapter combines song diffusion data with a social network of Top 40 stations. Although some stations are indeed extremely well-regarded (and therefore good candidates for opinion leadership), there is no correlation between a station's popularity and its typical add date. Such an outcome was predictable from the finding in chapter 2 that song diffusion is usually exogenous, but the chapter shows that even in the absence of label promotion efforts the song does not diffuse through the network.

Chapter 5 is a case study of the Dixie Chick's blacklist. Unlike the other chapters, the blacklist was an issue of how stations stopped playing music rather than how they started. Following a remark criticizing President Bush, the Dixie Chicks disappeared from the radio in just a few weeks. As in chapter 2, common explanations blaming this on large radio chains turn out to be fallacious. Rather, stations seemed to be responding to political considerations of their locations and of their formats.

The theme of format continues and expands in chapter 6. This chapter demonstrates the unusual pattern seen for crossover hits, which as usual spread exogenously in their home format but then spread endogenously in subsequent formats. This seems to reflect stations preferring to use genre conventions as a direct heuristic and then for dubious cases falling back on cascades of their peers. This raises the issue of how genres that do not fit in existing formats can ever become popular, so the chapter continues with the rise of reggaetón as a case study. Initially songs in the genre spread endogenously, but over time the genre developed a format niche within which its genre conventions were sufficiently accepted that songs could spread exogenously.

Overall we have a portrait of radio where the primary forces are genre conventions and record label promotions, with endogenous field-level dynamics having an occasional role when these primary forces are absent. In contrast, such issues as social networks between stations and corporate coordination of either adds or censorship are notable for their absence—notwithstanding the conventional wisdom about these forces among both researchers and members of the music industry. Some of these findings about pop music in the early years of the twenty-first century may generalize across time and to other cultural fields, but many of them are contingent to the nature of this field as it exists at the present time. The following sections will discuss these findings in more detail and attempt to extrapolate their relevance to the emerging media landscape.

7.2 Centralization and Distribution of Decision-making

One of the most common concerns about media is that large corporations will shape their content. This is commonly voiced in concerns that corporate ownership of a media outlet will translate into the outlet promoting the corporation's commercial and political interests— a kind of folk version of *The German Ideology*'s principle that "thus their ideas are the ruling ideas of the epoch."[29] Less dramatically, concerns over radio ownership specifically are often premised on the idea that corporate ownership of radio will squelch creativity and localism by imposing a standard set of programming brought into the local station from corporate headquarters.

What such fears miss is that it is one thing for a firm to own a property and another for the firm to control what goes on within that property. Corporate management certainly translates into appreciable control over strategic decisions like overall architecture issues and the general market niche the property will occupy. However, it is less likely that corporate management will micro-manage routine decisions. Consider the example of Sony, which bought Columbia Pictures and Columbia Records specifically to control their adoption of technical standards, and yet avoids any interference with routine creative decisions, even when those decisions involve hundreds of millions of dollars, as exemplified by the CEO's boast that:

> We in Tokyo don't have competence in film or music. We don't decide, and we don't give the green light to finance projects for Sony Music or Sony Pictures in the United States. One does not give the green light for *Spider Man* from Japan. The budget of the film was not presented for approval here. This decision was made entirely in the United States.[30]

The analyses in this book have emphasized routine decision-making within the constraints of a core strategy: should our pop music station play this particular pop song yet or wait awhile longer? While it seems that corporate management is indeed involved in decisions about big-picture issues like the viability of a format, more routine decisions about particular songs seem to be made locally. In chapter 2 we saw that the decision to adopt a song is made at the station level without even a faint influence of coordination at the corporate level. Thus, some widely reported unpleasant incidents notwithstanding, it seems that radio chains are not centralizing programming decisions on a systematic basis. Likewise, there is no support for the popular notion that corporate management of Clear Channel blacklisted the Dixie Chicks. Rather, stations seem to have each been responding individually to anti-Chicks activism. Even Cumulus, which did blacklist the Dixie Chicks at the corporate level from its Country stations, only did so once station-level decisions had already made the Country blacklist a fait accompli.

Although this book has found no evidence for corporate control of routine decisions in radio, strategic decisions tend to be made at the corporate level. Probably the biggest decision a radio station can make

101

is whether to continue programming in its format or flip to a new one, and if so, which. Analysis of this strategic issue (which sociologists call niche partitioning and economists call spatial competition) shows clear evidence of corporate influence. Within a local market, radio chains avoid duplicating formats. Across markets, corporate management applies lessons about niche viability learned in one market to their properties elsewhere.[31] When Clear Channel flipped some of their underperforming rock stations to the new "Hurban" hip-hop and reggaetón format, the decision was not made by individual station programmers or even general managers but by Alfredo Alonso, senior vice president for Hispanic radio.[32] Note though that while corporations may make strategic decisions for their properties, the various radio chains tend to make similar strategic decisions to one another, with giant radio chains like Clear Channel, Citadel, Cumulus, and CBS all having similarly diverse station portfolios.[33] This implies that even at the strategic level, the behavior of radio firms is considerably constrained by the environment—a point that both media executives and media critics forget only at their peril.

Thus, overall it appears that corporations make strategic decisions for their properties but delegate routine decisions within the boundaries established by the strategy. In the future, both aspects of this pattern should persist and even be exacerbated. Two trends characterize the emerging media landscape: on the one hand there is a shift from professionally curated broadcasting to automated narrowcasting, and on the other hand there is a renewed importance for creation of strategic alliances to leverage properties for corporate interests. Although seemingly contradictory, these trends apply at different levels and together should cement the current pattern that corporate media will decentralize and delegate (indeed, partially automate) routine decisions but treat architectural and licensing issues strategically. The issue of routinizing tactical decision-making to the point of automation is intertwined with a series of other issues in the next few sections and so will be discussed in those contexts. However, the strategic landscape of the media industry can be discussed in relative isolation.

Understanding the strategic issues in question in the emerging media landscape is best seen in contrast to the field's recent past. For most of the second half of the twentieth century the structure of the entertainment industry was characterized by a set of market conventions and regulations that encouraged arms-length transactions with relatively little transaction costs or holdout problems. Traditional radio in particular is a field where stations don't need anyone's permission.[34] Radio formats are not protected by intellectual property law and so radio stations can freely imitate their rivals. Similarly, the broadcasting of songs is subject to standard licensing rates so record labels, musicians, and music publishers cannot refuse broadcasters this key resource, although (as seen in chapter 3) stations can and do negotiate with labels for additional resources like live performances and promotional support. The artistic and business implications of a different licensing scheme can be seen by watching the transformation of hip-hop following a series of court cases, from *Grand Upright v. Warner* (1991) to *Bridgeport v. Dimension* (2005) that gave incumbent intellectual property holders holdout rights over sampling.[35] Overall, the environment facing emerging media is more similar to that of hip-hop musicians clearing samples than that of radio stations playing whatever they like and letting ASCAP/BMI collect the royalties. As such, corporate strategy is not merely a downstream issue of developing products that will appeal to consumers (egocentric uncertainty), but an upstream issue of securing access to resources (altercentric uncertainty).[36] Such a market violates the assumption of perfect competition found in simple models of supply and demand. Rather, exchange in this world will be of the sort described by theories of resource dependency and public choice, with firms seeking to favorably shape their relation to the environment through mergers, strategic alliances, and political machinations.[37]

Various structural features of the mass media in the late twentieth century that facilitated relatively simple exchange at arms length have recently been attenuated. Among these was anti-trust policy against vertical integration, to the benefit of new entrants who might otherwise be locked out of exchange. The Supreme Court case *US v. Paramount* (1948) ruled against the old practice of block-booking, a system in which studios would sell bundles of good and bad films to theaters, and forced the film industry onto a spot market for theatrical exhibition.[38] Similarly, the FCC's 1970 finance and syndication ("fin-syn") rule held that broadcasters could not have an equity stake in the syndication rights to content, which in effect meant that networks could only directly produce ephemera (e.g., news and sports) for which there is little or no appetite for reruns. Since the scripted content that characterizes prime time doesn't turn a profit until it goes into reruns, the networks were forced to rely on a spot market for television series where independent producers like Carsey-Werner were fully competitive with the television divisions of major corporations like Time Warner.[39] Common carrier rules characterized the telecommunications industry, including in such business-to-business aspects as backbone networks for the long-distance transmission of network and syndicated content to broadcasters. Such common carriage became especially strong when the federal government broke up AT&T's telephone monopoly in 1982,

103

largely over its reluctance to inter-operate with the long-distance carrier MCI.[40] Similarly, the technical architecture of the Internet traditionally gives all traffic equal priority, meaning that websites and other Internet content providers needn't negotiate access with telecoms.

All of these policies have been reversed or superseded by new developments. The FCC repealed fin-syn in 1993 which had the substantial benefit of creating two (briefly three) new broadcast television networks but has largely pushed independent producers out of scripted prime time programming, as the studios and networks have moved toward vertical integration.[41] Common carriage is under threat by two business trends. First, the same digital convergence that was made possible by the Telecommunications Act of 1996 gives telecoms a strong incentive to block Internet services that compete with their telephone services (e.g., Skype) or television services (e.g., Netflix and BitTorrent). While few telecoms have actually blocked such competing services, the content providers (as well as media reform activists) were sufficiently afraid of the possibility that they convinced the FCC to reaffirm common carrier principles in late 2010 with the adoption of "net neutrality." Second, the open Internet is increasingly being replaced by "walled garden" systems like Facebook and the iTunes App Store in which a company brokers access between its users and developers. Although these walled gardens provide fairly wide latitude to third-party content developers, they inhibit competition over audience ratings and advertising.[42] These two great walled gardens have recently clashed with Facebook's refusal to interoperate with the iTunes Ping social networking feature, much to the detriment of the latter.

Another important means for promoting arms-length transactions is the "first sale" doctrine in intellectual property law. This means that once a copyright holder sells a copy of a work in the primary market, the purchaser has an unencumbered right to resell or rent that copy of the work. The first sale doctrine is an important form of bundling intellectual property rights because it allows pass-through from the primary to the secondary market, and by extension facilitates innovation. However, it has failed to make the transition to the Internet because first sale allows transferring a work but not copying a work, and in digital media this distinction is meaningless.[43] The result is that the lack of an effective first sale doctrine has made the creation of digital services to recirculate old content exponentially more difficult. This can be seen most clearly with Netflix, which under "first sale" had the legal right to provide a mail-order rental service for physical DVDs, whereas for its streaming video service it has had to negotiate a series of agreements with rights-holders. As a result, for the first few years of operation Netflix's streaming library had a much smaller number of much less desirable titles than did its mail order service, and it was only in 2009 that the streaming library even began to approach the mail-order library in quality and scope. Similarly, when UCLA attempted to move some of its library's video holdings to a "Video Furnace" streaming service so students could watch videos from their dorm rooms or faculty from their offices rather than visiting the undergraduate library's basement, the trade group Association for Information Media and Equipment sent the university a cease and desist letter. While UCLA's counsel ultimately determined that the university was protected by a special educational exemption, two things are noteworthy about the incident. First, the university's streaming service was sufficiently dubious that the university shut it down for a month while assessing their legal standing, whereas the legality of circulating tangible books or DVDs is iron-clad. Second, the exemption does not apply to commercial services like Netflix or even non-profits in fields other than education. Another issue where digital libraries have been obstructed by legal difficulties is Google Books, a project in which the company endeavored to scan and index (but not recirculate the full text of) the University of Michigan library. This provoked a set of lawsuits from the Authors Guild and the Association of American Publishers that delayed the project until Google reached a settlement.

The increasing extent to which incumbent intellectual property rights-holders can exert holdout rights is important because this gives incumbents leverage against emergent media in a context when they may have contrary interests. Historically, "[t]he process of media evolution does not occur without substantial resistance, as industry sectors engage in various efforts to preserve their established positions, whether by attacking the emerging media through legal or economic means, or by attempting to adopt the characteristics of the new, threatening medium."[44] Similarly, Wu (2010) refers to the "Kronos Effect," in which incumbent media attempt to swallow up emerging media, often successfully as with network radio's control of television. This can involve lawsuits and regulatory capture, but also mergers and strategic alliances to lock up access to resources.

One such issue is the interdependence of content providers and the providers of technical architecture or distribution systems (an issue sometimes known as the hardware-software synergy). Such dependencies are resolved through mergers or alliances. Most famously, following its failure to establish Betamax as the standard for videotape in the 1980s, Sony became convinced that its ability to establish future technical standards depended on controlling a substantial content library with which to prime the pump and so purchased (in separate transactions) Columbia Records and Columbia Pictures.[45] In part on the strength of the Columbia film library, Sony was able to establish first the DVD and later the Blu-Ray as standards for video players.[46] However, control of content does not provide total power to set technical standards, as seen by Sony's failure to successfully launch the MiniDisc, Super Audio CD, or ATRAC3 digital audio codec despite its use of the Columbia Records library to seed the use of these formats. The next looming entertainment format war looks to be over streaming video Digital Rights Management, with Apple and Disney backing KeyChest as opposed to the Ultraviolet standard backed by most other electronics and entertainment companies.

Following a similar logic as Sony had before it of vertical integration with content to attain control over technical channels, the cable operator Comcast recently acquired the entertainment conglomerate NBC Universal. Here the issue is mostly the cable set-top box. One of Comcast's goals is trying to draw more viewers to video-on-demand through the set-top box by closing the four-month window between theatrical release and release on DVD and video-on-demand. Further shrinking or even eliminating the window appeals to film studios (who would economize on marketing and mitigate piracy) and cable operators (who would be more competitive with theaters) but has been militantly opposed by movie theaters who routinely threaten to boycott any film with a tighter window.[47] Comcast seems to think that vertical integration (and perhaps an alliance with Time Warner, which is in a similar position) would give it the power to force a war with the theatrical exhibition industry to expand the scope of content consumed through the cable box.

Comcast's other strategic interest is to keep the cable box from losing consumers. Cable companies see a risk that consumers will "cut the cord" as cheap Internet video becomes attractive relative to expensive cable subscriptions. With the increasing availability of video content from YouTube, Netflix, iTunes, Amazon On Demand, Hulu, and BitTorrent, the cable television industry fears that it will suffer similar problems as the newspaper and music industries have already suffered.[48] These fears are particularly exacerbated by devices that allow consumers to easily watch Internet content on a television rather than computer screen—most notably the Roku, Apple TV, Google TV, Boxee Box, and various Internet-enabled Blu-Ray players, HDTVs, and video game consoles. The cable industry has fought back by employing tactics designed to keep television content primarily available through cable and not allow television content streamed on the Internet to be reimported back onto a television screen. For instance, after seeing demonstrations of Boxee software running on a set-top box, Fox and NBC executives demanded that Hulu blacklist the Boxee user-agent string. About 18 months later, Hulu launched the set-top device-compatible "Hulu Plus" service at $8 a month. The logic of Hulu Plus seems to be as much about preserving the old business model as it is about raising revenue through the new one, much as the pay-wall for WSJ.com has always been more about preserving the print edition of the *Journal* than it is about revenue for the website. Although NBC had been skittish about Internet video well before Comcast began courting it, part of the appeal of the merger seems to be that it would reinforce NBC's will to keep its primary loyalties with cable distribution. Overall, Comcast's strategic goal is to both extend and preserve the cash cow that is the monthly cable subscription, and it sees vertical integration with a major content provider as key to achieving this goal. It is worth noting, though, that the conditions regulators attached to the merger limit Comcast's actions that might serve this purpose.[49]

Directly opposed to Comcast's strategy to use vertical integration to preserve and extend the cable television market is Apple's strategy to use strategic alliances to disrupt it. In 2006, Apple unveiled the first Apple TV but referred to the product as a "hobby," then made a more aggressive push with its release of a cheaper second-generation device in 2010. Concurrent with the second-generation device, Apple announced a 99 cent 720p resolution streaming video market. For users who watch only about an hour of television a day, this would be a much cheaper option than a cable subscription and thus provide an incentive to cut the cord. Perhaps not surprisingly, CBS and NBC were wary of this potentially disruptive innovation and vowed to stay out of the Apple TV market. However, ABC and Fox did enter this streaming video market, at least provisionally. As discussed above, NBC Universal's new corporate parent prefers that its content stay out of such disruptive markets, but this is not to say that ABC and Fox's decisions to enter the Apple TV rental market were based solely on the attractions of its revenue potential. The CEO of Apple, Steve Jobs, was a board member and the single largest shareholder in Disney, and business analysts attribute the firms' cooperation on Internet television to this interlock.[50] Similarly, the business press attributed Fox's cooperation with the Apple TV to Rupert Murdoch's enthusiasm for using the iPad as a platform for Newscorp's newspapers.[51]

Taken together these changes make strategic alliances at the corporate level more important. In many ways we have a return to the pre-1955 cultural system described in Peterson and Berger (1975), and not just because *American Idol, Glee,* and the Ashman/Menken Disney films have re-popularized Broadway style entertainment. Rather, we are seeing a system where the core of the culture industries is dominated by large corporations in strategic alliance with each other for control of intellectual property rights, leverage of publicity, and the establishment of technical platforms.

7.3 The Struggle to Control Publicity

As described in the introduction to this book, the production of culture paradigm arguably began with the article "Processing Fads and Fashions: An Organization-Set Analysis of Cultural Industry Systems."[52] This article emphasizes the boundary-spanning processes between original artists, cultural distributors, surrogate consumers, and consumers. It describes cultural markets as a sequence of gatekeeping processes at each point in the pipeline from artist to consumer and gives greatest emphasis to the boundaries between distributors and surrogate consumers, whom the distributors co-opt instead of engaging in prohibitively expensive direct advertising efforts.

The production of culture tradition has maintained an emphasis on such boundary-spanning processes ever since. Work immediately following Hirsch (1972) similarly emphasized the upstream and downstream boundaries with distributors, as seen in such issues as how exogenous shocks disrupting embedded ties with surrogate consumers led incumbent distributor market share to collapse and how boundary-spanning work is often delegated to entrepreneurial brokers who are either independent contractors or so autonomous and mobile that they might as well be.[53] More recent work tends to be more cognitive than structural but has maintained similar emphases on the boundary-spanning of distributors as the key locus of action in cultural markets.[54] Perhaps the strongest theoretical case for the importance of boundary-spanning in general, and distributor relations with surrogate consumers in particular, comes from Neuman's *Future of the Mass Audience* (1991) which notes that barriers to entry for production costs and distribution costs could be (and in retrospect have proven to be) ameliorated by technology, but audience attention is inherently scarce and so barriers to entry through promotion are an eternal issue.

The historical and quantitative analyses in chapter 3 have shown that the radio field is profoundly shaped by its relationship with the record industry. Most pop songs exhibit a diffusion pattern consistent with emanation from a central source rather than any kind of endogenous dynamic. The two major exceptions are the rare songs that become hits without being an official single (such as "My Humps," discussed in chapter 4) and songs crossing over between genres (as discussed in chapter 6). Overall, though, the pattern is of central coordination, and we have good reason to suspect that the actors responsible for the coordination are record labels because in chapter 2 we excluded the possibilities that the pattern is driven by record release dates or radio chains. Furthermore, the diffusion pattern consistent with central coordination is especially pronounced for songs shown in court to have involved payola and especially weak during immediate threats of policy scrutiny. Despite recurring efforts to stamp it out, there has been a major payola scandal every 14 or 15 years, just as, generations earlier, vaudeville was co-opted by song-pluggers from sheet music publishers.

None of this is to say that radio programming is an auction. Rather, payola is just the extreme form of a continuum that spans from advice accepted purely for its intrinsic wisdom, to subtle gift exchange and brokerage by indies, all the way to explicit quid pro quos for cash, promotional budgets, drugs, sex, or intellectual property rights. Similarly, qualitative interviews with radio programmers identify an "industry" or "synergistic" approach to programming based on relationships with record labels that emphasizes the extent to which the record labels provide valuable advice and resources that can benefit the station and listeners.[55] In these interviews, programmers almost always claim that resources change hands only when the programming decision was already made. Even if we assume that these qualitative respondents are engaging in face-saving spin to make their behavior seem more legitimate (and legal), their reports have to be taken seriously as evidence that (at least since the RIAA's 1986 reforms) some very large proportion of radio interactions with labels have fallen short of payola, or at least were so subtle as to make plausible the self-deception that one's choices were not being swayed.

We have every reason to believe that the emerging media environment will involve efforts by distributors to influence surrogate consumers. However, while certain features of how such boundary-spanning occurs in radio will generalize to other media, some aspects are peculiar to the medium. One of the most peculiar features of radio is that (under US Code 47 § 317) when a payment is made to a station to induce a broadcast, the station will make an announcement disclosing the payment during the broadcast. There are two things that are unusual about this requirement: that the linear nature of the medium makes it conspicuous (and therefore burdensome), and that it applies at all. Radio is essentially a completely linear, single-channel medium with no place for discreet "fine print" disclosures. Thus, disclosing a payment on the air requires interrupting the broadcast to read a disclosure. Even though such a disclosure could be just a brief sentence, radio stations don't like to interrupt music with talk. This is especially true if that talk might spoil the premise of the interaction with the listener that the music is chosen on the basis of its appeal to the fan community. In contrast, television (which is also subject to the payola law) traditionally has had no trouble complying in large part because it is a richer medium, able to combine sound, moving image, and text. Many television programs, especially game shows and reality shows, feature paid product shots which they disclose as part of the closing credits—a much less intrusive form of disclosure than having a disk jockey read "this song was brought to you by" Essentially all emerging media are more similar to television than radio in this respect. Even Internet and satellite "radio" contain fairly conspicuous text channels through which a station could make "fine print" disclosures of comparable visibility, as seen on television closing credits.[56] Thus, the technical difficulties of disclosing promotional considerations are essentially unique to radio.

There is also the fact that terrestial radio and television have a unique place in American law following the historical contingencies of their origins. Radio and television broadcasting is based on a model of public ownership of the broadcasting spectrum to which the broadcaster has a theoretically revocable license. Similarly, the legal doctrine of "scarcity" (*Red Lion v. FCC* 1969) holds that since there is a finite amount of radio and television spectrum to be allocated, the government has more power over these media than the First Amendment would allow for any other medium (*Miami Herald v. Tornillo* 1974). Together, the legal and political framing of "public airwaves" as a sort of "scarce" fief delegated to broadcasters allows much more intrusive regulation over broadcasting than would be conscionable in other media. In this context, a moral panic over rigged quiz shows and bribed disk jockeys made it easy for Congress, the bureaucracy, and the courts alike to see these scandals not through the frame of freedom of the press but merely as mischievous tenants deserving to be held to a more stringent lease. In contrast, neither nominal public ownership nor scarcity are relevant issues for most emerging media. The Internet is not usually understood as involving a commons of any sort, and the idea that there is a scarcity of websites is absurd.

Overall, legal requirements to disclose sponsorship should prove less likely to be imposed on emerging media and less onerous to comply with if they were than is the case in radio. Even though not legally required to, many emerging media voluntarily comply with similar standards. For instance, the "Featured" videos on the main page of YouTube are chosen without sponsorship, although YouTube does include clearly marked "promoted videos" in search results. Still, videos are promoted, both in the YouTube search results and via advertising elsewhere on the Internet. An analysis of all the videos on YouTube over the course of several months found that videos that became popular tended to be characterized by internal influence or external influence, although the study did not attempt to identify correlates for these patterns.[57] Even more intriguingly, analyses of streaming videos posted by advertisers to YouTube and elsewhere have found that most of these videos have a large initial burst of views and some (but not all) show s-curve growth thereafter.[58] The inference we can draw is that "viral marketing" involves a substantial amount of external influence, a pattern similar to that in the seminal work of Bass (1969).

Although chapter 3 emphasized attempts by record labels to purchase the cooperation of radio stations, the case of "phoner campaigns" shows that they are not above deceiving them. The closest analogy to "phoners" in emerging media would be "sock-puppeting," in which one writes a positive user review of one's own product or comment about one's own ideas while pretending to be a third party. A much more important issue is "search engine optimization" or "Google bombing," in which one games the algorithms used by surrogate consumers. An early version of this was a search war waged between the Church of Scientology and its critics over whether scientology.org or xenu.net would be the top hit in search engines for the query "scientology."[59] Among other things, the war involved Scientology distributing CD-ROMs with website-building kits to its members on L. Ron Hubbard's birthday in 1998, which succeeded in building approximately 7,000 websites, all of which linked to scientology.org and other websites run by Scientology.[60] This incident illustrates the main techniques of search engine optimization, which is to increase the number of incoming links targeting a website. Usually though the link-farming websites are generated automatically by computer scripts rather than with direct human cooperation, as in the Scientology case. Search engine operators are aware of these techniques and continually try to improve the robustness of their results to such gaming, for instance by increasing the weight of the transitivity parameter in status metrics or by identifying and ignoring clusters of otherwise isolated web pages. Indeed, Google's implementation of PageRank was successful in part because it was less vulnerable than earlier search engines to the simple trick of loading up documents with common search terms (usually in the meta-text).

Overall the emerging media should continue to see distributors attempt to influence surrogate consumers as the most cost-effective way to reach the ultimate consumers. Some of this will continue to take the form of payment, but the combination of less onerous disclosure and a different set of historical contingencies will reframe such payments as legitimate promotion rather than illegitimate payola. Unsavory distributor behavior will continue, but as surrogate consumers increasingly shift from human curation to algorithms, this will mostly be a matter of deceiving the computer rather than corrupting the human gatekeeper.

7.4 Structures of Salient Information

The opinion leadership hypothesis holds that much diffusion flows through networks, and actors with central locations in the network therefore have strong influence on diffusion.[61] In chapter 4 we saw that participants in the pop music field believe that some radio stations are opinion leaders, but the analyses in this book found no evidence that these stations actually "break" pop songs. This seems to be because in most cases diffusion is over-specified by label promotional efforts. In those cases where a song accidentally becomes a single, the mechanism seems to be field-level generalized diffusion, in part because this is how salient information is organized. However, both of these issues are contingent and we can imagine counterfactual media landscapes where different structural conditions facilitate different diffusion mechanisms, including network contagion and even opinion leadership.

The issue is not that the network structure of radio fails the scope condition for opinion leadership identified by Watts and Dodds (2007) that opinion leadership requires strong hubs. In fact, the distribution of radio station centrality does follow a power-law distribution consistent with a preferential attachment network formation model. Rather, the issue is that songs do not seem to diffuse through the social network of stations at all. For most songs diffusion is over-specified by the effects of genre conventions and record label promotion and songs simply spread too quickly to be much affected by peer adoptions. Similarly, exogenous efforts are common in many fields. Two medical diffusion studies came to different results as to the importance of opinion leadership, and the difference between them appears to be that in one case the pharmaceutical company did not have an intensive conventional marketing campaign.[62] More broadly, we can say that another scope condition for opinion leadership is the absence of strong exogenous forces that might swamp the slow-building effects of peer diffusion.

In those cases where radio stations clearly are imitating their peers rather than taking their cues from record labels, they seem not to be imitating their immediate peers who they report as network alters so much as the aggregation of their peers. The issue is not so much that social networks do not matter, but that it does matter what information is salient and traditionally information is most often presented at the field level.[63] When field-level information is more salient than the behavior of particular alters, the result is generalized information cascades rather than contagious diffusion directly through the network graph.[64] In a large-scale experiment, behavior responded weakly to discreetly presented popularity information but strongly to conspicuous popularity information.[65] Similarly, record labels tend to rely on the *Billboard* chart more than their own sales data for getting a big picture of the music industry, to the extent that they were surprised by the results of "the Soundscan revolution" (which made the charts more accurately reflect sales).[66] Even when people are aware of biases or limitations to summary data, they tend to reify and act upon naive readings.[67] Thus, even if people are aware of the complexity of underlying reality or alternative interpretations, the salient summary presentations of data can exert great influence on behavior in the field, including reactivity whereby actors change their behavior in attempts to game the data summary. The power of institutionalized forms of information is perhaps best expressed by Espeland and Stevens:

> Berger & Luckmann argue that socially constructed meaning becomes more fact-like when it is objectified or reified, that is, when social practices are organized to sustain the appearance that meaning stands outside of individual subjectivity, as part of the world (1966, 47–92; Berger, 1967, 3–24). In keeping with this insight, we argue that as commensuration gets built into the practical organization of labor and resources, it becomes more taken for granted and more constitutive of what it measures. Thus, however arbitrary, the Chicago Board of Trade's standardized grades of grain quality became ever more constitutive of what they measured as the number of parties who used the measures grew: not only farmers and merchants, but also elevator operators, banks, the trade press, and ultimately the state legislature.[68]

That is, the ways we structure information take on importance in of themselves and can structure social action including such diffusion processes as information cascades.

In the pop music field, both airplay and sales data are available in fine-grained form, but the raw station-level or point-of-sale-level data are much less salient than the charts aggregating information at the level of the format. Similarly, "best-seller" lists of various kinds structure many fields beyond the music industry and are often directly salient to consumers, as with regular newspaper features showing the best-selling books or weekend movie box office.[69] Furthermore, industry gatekeepers may use best-seller information for decisions such as what songs to play in the "countdown" or what products to keep in inventory.

113

Thus, both directly and indirectly presenting information as a list sorted by popularity can promote cumulative advantage.

However, there is no necessary reason why information needs to be aggregated in this way. With the growth of digital technology, we have seen the development of alternative ways to structure information.[70] The less radical approaches still structure information in a single rank order but find alternatives to mere quantity for sorting the list. The more radical approaches do away with a single list (or a handful of lists broken out by genre) and find ways to present information customized to appeal to the particular user.

Recently, eigenvector centrality measures have become popular, most notably the PageRank algorithm at the core of the Google search engine. Although more sophisticated than traditional best-seller lists, these measures are conceptually related in that they produce a single rank order that is proportional to popularity, albeit as weighted by the popularity of those doing the choosing, ad infinitum.[71] In effect, these metrics recursively measure status and arrange information to make high-status information more salient. Increasing use of such measures should create an opinion leader effect, not because members of the field necessarily look directly to highly central actors in the network, but because the field is attentive to a summary index of information which heavily weights the "opinion leader's" contribution. In such a scenario, opinion leaders would indeed exert great influence over the field but only as a self-fulfilling prophecy, making the opinion leadership hypothesis an exercise in Barnesian performativity.[72] When we believe we are seeing what Podolny (2001) calls "pipes" in the form of websites imitating websites they link to, it may really be that PageRank is serving as a "prism" that makes such popular websites more salient to everyone. That is not to say that arranging information in such a way is undesirable. Certainly, anyone old enough to remember how painful web search was in the 1990s will appreciate what a tremendous benefit PageRank provided to Internet users.

More radical approaches to presenting information reject the idea of a single list, whether sorted by popularity or status, but customize information to the particular user. The simplest way to do this is to rely on demographic information to make Bayesian inferences about the salience of information.[73] More popular are various collaborative filtering algorithms which are often presented to users as "recommendations" by such companies as Amazon, Netflix, and TiVo. These algorithms use factor analysis and related models to find different taste niches so as to identify product choices that may be unpopular in general but are relevant to the particular user. Unfortunately, these algorithms can choke on sparse data, so they often give inaccurate results when dealing with items that have been rated by few users or providing results to users who have rated few items. In part to handle such issues, some newer engines, such as the Music Genome Project used by Pandora Radio, code traits of the object (e.g., a song's tempo) so that inferences of salience are made on the basis of the user's taste for kinds of objects rather than the similarity of the user's past choices to those of other users. In effect such systems blur the line between collaborative filtering and genre schema.

Recent years have also seen the increasing salience of information through technologically mediated social networks. The popularity and user-friendliness of blogging (e.g., Wordpress), micro-blogging (e.g., Twitter), and social networking sites (e.g., Facebook) allow users to make their choices conspicuous. These choices are then available to alters (usually called "friends"), either as discrete streams of information by source or with all of the user's subscriptions interpolated together into a feed.[74] This creates a style of information flow closely matching that assumed by cohesive contagion models of diffusion—which is no accident since many of these services are explicitly modeled on social network theory—and thus provides a way of making information diffuse via cohesion rather than by information cascades, as is implicit in most other styles of presenting information. Marketers have aggressively adopted the social networking trend. In his book on recent developments in advertising, Phil Napoli notes:

> [A]udiences today engage in a wide range of activities that assist in the marketing of products, ranging from self-producing commercials to engaging in online word-of-mouth and endorsements (via blogs, tweets, etc.), to integrating brand messages into their own communication platforms. ... Contemporary marketing and advertising strategies increasingly focus on taking the value of consumer "word of mouth" to entirely new levels and developing new methods for facilitating and encouraging consumers to do the work of marketers and advertisers in the dissemination of brand messages.[75]

The advertising trade journal *Ad Age* publishes an average of almost two articles a week about Facebook and/or Twitter and recently noted that for some marketers these social media platforms are eclipsing ordinary websites.[76] Particularly relevant to music is that in 2010 Apple deprecated iTune's collaborative filtering algorithm ("Genius") in favor of a social networking tool ("Ping") that lets artists and users micro-blog, endorse songs and concerts, and follow the contributions of other users and artists through an interpolated "recent activity" feed.

These changing technologies and business practices are restructuring the nature of salient information. Traditionally information was arranged by lists sorted by popularity or status, with the implication that this promotes generalized threshold patterns of diffusion.[77] An emerging trend is for these traditional lists of information to co-exist with information customized to match the user's taste profile or social network alters—styles of information presentation more compatible with true contagious diffusion. Thus, it is entirely plausible that this book's finding that music diffusion (at least among radio stations) is not at all driven by social networks will prove to be contingent on the current nature of the way the music industry processes information, and in the future diffusion will be increasingly driven by social networks. Furthermore, the line is blurring between market information and the market itself. That is, rather than us as consumers listening to radio stations with programming informed by pop charts, we are increasingly relying on such things as links to streaming video clips embedded in our various feeds. Nonetheless, even if technology makes it possible to see information from the perspective of ego-centric networks, most people will retain some interest in a mass culture—with all that implies for the continued power of major content providers, the curatorial functions of gatekeepers, and the salience of aggregated information.[78]

7.5 Genre

One of the defining features of art forms in general, and of pop music in particular, is how they are defined and even constituted by genre.[79] This is especially true of radio, where much market information is arranged by genre. Furthermore, as seen in chapter 6, radio stations seem to evaluate songs by genre conventions. When a song spreads through its initial format, stations adopt it without regard to their peers, most likely on the basis of its genre fit. However, when a song crosses over to another format, stations show influence of peer adoption as the intrinsic qualities of the song are insufficient to motivate adoption. Similarly, early on in reggaetón's popularity it mostly spread following the crossover pattern because it lacked many radio stations who considered the new genre to be a close fit with their format. It was only with the spread of "Hurban" stations (a process that was itself based on peer dynamics) that reggaetón had a large number of stations comfortable enough with the genre to adopt new songs within it on the merits, without waiting for peer validation of the particular song.

In the future, genre is likely to become more complicated, with implications that are hard to extrapolate for how pop songs become popular. Since the mid-1950s, we have seen a long-term trend toward ever more fine-grained genre distinctions being institutionalized in radio formats. Much of this is made possible by various technological and market changes that make it possible to target narrower niches of consumers.[80] In radio this genre entropy was held in check by the width of the FM dial, but such constraints aren't felt in digital media. In satellite radio the trend is less to provide strictly redundant offerings (e.g., ten stations all playing hip-hop) but to develop even more fine-grained distinctions (e.g., one station playing 1980s hip-hop, another playing dirty south hip-hop, etc.). Similarly, "hybrid digital" technology allows traditional FM radio stations to offer a second band, and many of them give this second station a slightly different genre identity.

Of course any type of Internet distribution creates essentially unlimited space for product variety. This then leads to the problem of how users can make sense of the available offerings, and genre is often seen as a solution. The sheer volume of offerings though would make it such that a broad level genre would still have tens of thousands of entries, so genre labels are too broad to be informative for a browsing consumer who wishes to avoid being swamped by choices. To keep the number of entries per genre reasonably small, some systems differentiate smaller sub-genres. Early music websites, such as the original version of mp3.com, would have hundreds of infinitesimally differentiated genres. It is not that these absurdly narrow genres pre-existed the website and the musicians created the music to fit these conventions, but that the website invented and imposed these genres to make some sense out of a tremendous variety of music. In the 1990s, music databases relied on the user community (e.g., CDDB) or experts (e.g., allmusic.com) to hand-code genre labels. Slightly later, computer scientists experimented with fully automated computerized genre coding that would directly code audio files, but the results were both insufficiently specific and insufficiently reliable.[81] Since then the Music Genome Project has emerged as a hybrid form, relying on human experts to hand-code a long list of musical attributes and then allowing a computerized algorithm to identify patterns from the coded attributes.

Similarly, Netflix helps users browse by genre, and its website "Genre" list has a list of 20 relatively clear and meaningful genres like "Documentaries," "Comedies," and "Dramas." Click on any one of these genres and there will be a further list of 20 or so sub-genres. Some of these genres are meaningful in their own right, such as "Westerns" or "Heist Films" as sub-genre of "Action & Adventure." There is also a cross-classifying "Alternative Genre" schema of "Feel-good," "Family-friendly," and "Dark," and a system of hybrid genre schema that is prominent in the various interfaces for Netflix's streaming service that

117

consists of such categories as "Feel-good Talking-Animal TV Shows," "Fight the System Movies," and "Mind-bending Supernatural Movies from the 1980s." These were almost certainly not understood by anyone to be categories until a Netflix staffer had to come up with a name for a list of films spit out by a latent class algorithm.

Perhaps not surprisingly, these narrow labels are arbitrary, and when multiple websites or other systems classify the same artist or cultural object they seldom agree.[82] Any two people would probably agree that Franz Ferdinand is a rock band and *Reno 911* a television comedy, but it would be surprising were these two people, when asked for more specificity, to both describe Franz Ferdinand as a "New Wave/Post-Punk Revival" band (as does AllMusic) or *Reno 911* a "Raunchy Workplace TV Show" (as does Netflix). Such narrow labels are not especially meaningful, which introduces the issue of categorical uncertainty—a problem that reduces the appeal of entertainment.[83]

Given the problems of coding labels, many services have moved away from narrow genre labels. Most notably, the main music page of the iTunes store contains no explicit references to genre schema. The front page lists new releases, single and album top 10 charts, "what's hot," playlists created by celebrities, discounted albums, etc., but no references to anything like "Top Hip-Hop Albums," "Browse by Genre," or the like. Overall the prevailing assumption of the site is that there is a single mass culture. It is only after one hits the "page down" button twice that one sees anything approaching a genre schema, the "Genius Recommendations": offerings that Apple's collaborative filtering engine estimates are similar to the songs you already listen to. That is, the iTunes Store has essentially given up on recognizing or creating genres as an important way to display information. Rather than identifying categories into which an artist or artwork falls, iTunes emphasizes arranging them by analogy to other artists and artworks. Other services, such as Pandora Internet radio, Vevo streaming videos, and Amazon's MP3 download store, offer browsing by genre, but give equal or more emphasis to presenting similar songs to whatever particular song one happens to have selected. For instance, to a create a "station" in Pandora, one enters an artist to use a seed value and the station is thereafter referred to as "[Artist's Name] Radio," even though it branches out to include other artists similar to the seed artist.

To the extent that such schema continue to be institutionalized, this implies a radical reconceptualization of genre. Genre is traditionally conceived of as what quantitative methodologists would call a nominal or categorical variable. While it is often difficult to agree to what category or categories a particular object belongs, it is nonetheless meaningful that the categories have names and in principle exist sui generis of the particular artists or art works falling in these categories.[84] In the newer emerging conception of genre, the names for genres fall out entirely. Genre goes from being a set of fuzzy and overlapping categories to an irreducibly continuous set of multi-dimensional distances derived from a a massive vector of content attributes or a bipartite graph of consumers and objects. To the extent that such irreducibly fuzzy conceptions of genre become more institutionalized, it suggests potentially dramatic changes for the nature of cultural production.

When any given thing is understood as a member of a category, fields will punish hybrid forms. In the extreme case, particular market actors are tasked with responsibility for particular categories with the consequence that interstitial or hybrid activity gets less attention and resources. The net effect is to give categorical schema the quality of coercive isomorphism and reduce the frequency of hybrid objects in the field.[85] Contrariwise, if genre is re-conceptualized from a categorical distinction to a continuous one, then the concept of hybrid form becomes less meaningful.[86] In a system with such a flexible genre system we might imagine that the "categorical imperative" grows weaker and hybridity becomes more common. Such an outcome should not be overstated as it is a contingency of the shift to a new genre system and this is likely to occur only partially. In particular, any shift is likely to be more important to the consumer side than to the producer side. It is in the nature of human cognition that human gatekeepers deciding how to allocate scarce resources for big budget endeavors, such as television and films, will be more comfortable thinking in terms of categories and may penalize proposals for hybrid forms.[87] However, systems where computers present customized streams of information to individual consumers will be, and in fact already are, closely characterized by multidimensional and continuous alternatives to categorical genre. This will have the effect of promoting a consumer media consumption experience that fills in the gaps between categories.

7.6 The Emerging Structure of Popular Culture Industries in the Twenty-first Century

Although radio is a medium in (gradual) decline, we can still learn from it and apply its lessons to those media that are displacing it. Indeed, the same digital technologies that are displacing radio let us understand the old medium better than ever before. This irony is seen most clearly and concretely in the "Shazam" smartphone app, which gives ordinary users access to the same technology that underlies the monitored airplay databases.

The emerging media are different from the extant forms in many ways. Most obviously, true mass media have been partially replaced by narrowcasting and we are now taking this one step further with mass customization. Other changes are more subtle but just as important. For instance, new styles of presenting information blur genre distinctions, and social media has the performative potential to strengthen the effects of social network contagion. Nonetheless, there are likely to be many continuities with existing media and it would be a mistake to over-estimate changes. The single most common fallacy applied to technological change is to assume that it will be a great egalitarian leveler. This is simply false because there is a scarcity of human attention and controlling it can be a barrier to entry.[88] Furthermore, people generally *like* mass culture, which not only has higher production values but also benefits from information cascades and network externalities.[89]

One likely change is that cultural distributors like record labels will find it harder to co-opt and control popular taste, and climbing the chart will become somewhat more endogenous than it currently is. Although both tastemakers and grassroots cumulative advantage can have the end result of a few superstars clearly dominating the rest of the field, it is almost by definition vastly more difficult to shape grassroots developments than to influence a relatively small group of tastemakers. While cultural distributors will likely develop reasonably successful strategies for guiding grassroots trends to their advantage, they will almost certainly not be as good at this as they currently are at managing a relatively small number of tastemakers. While reducing the influence of distributors may sound very democratic, both theory and experimental evidence show that grassroots allocation of success tends to be only loosely coupled to quality.[90] Thus, the cultural landscape of the future may be just as concentrated but more stochastic and even less meritocratic as we see a decline of the curatorial power of elite gatekeepers. In other words, a world where songs become hits through appearing on the "most downloaded" list or being tweeted rather than through the judgment of professional gatekeepers is probably a world with more hits like "My Humps."

The transition from mass media with human curation to mass customization by algorithm and a heightened salience of information from one's own alters may create fundamental changes for the interrelationship of different aspects of the culture industries. These changes should be felt most profoundly in processes between role-sets rather than in the differences between occupants of similar roles. For instance, the changing nature of how distributors promote to surrogate consumers should be of vastly more interest than comparing one distributor to another. Identifying such structural changes (or for that matter, continuities) in how the culture industries work requires taking a step back from looking too closely at how various actors relate to any one cultural object in order to look for general patterns in how cultural objects move through the culture industry.

APPENDIX A

DATASETS

Monitored Airplay Data

Most of the analyses in this book are based on Mediabase. This database relies on monitored airplay in which Mediabase itself records which songs were played on the radio. Broadcast Data Systems and MediaGuide provide similar services. All of these monitored airplay services contrast with earlier systems of "reporting" stations where programmers would tell *Billboard* what songs they had been playing. The shift to monitored airplay is part of a broader shift in the media measurement industry since 1990 from techniques that rely on human recall to more accurate "passive monitoring" systems that are less vulnerable to both accidental cognitive biases and deliberate corruption (Anand and Peterson, 2000; Napoli, 2003, 2011).

Mediabase monitors most of the commercial FM radio stations in Arbitron rated markets. Arbitron markets are roughly comparable to the Census Bureau's concept of a Metropolitan Statistical Area. Mediabase includes some music video channels and satellite radio stations, but about 97 percent of the monitored stations are traditional terrestrial radio. Note that MTV typically adopts after the median CHR station and thus music video is not driving the external influence pattern described in chapter 2. Because Mediabase's panel has been expanding over time, in many cases a song began to spread through radio before a station was first observed. This presents the possibility of left-censorship, where the onset of observation can be easily confused with the onset of behavior. To avoid this problem I base analyses of each song only on stations that were already in the Mediabase panel before that song's first spin.

One of the main ways to read Mediabase is with a "song history" query, which lists every station that has ever played a song and (among other things) gives the date that the station "first played" the song. Most of the analyses in the book rely on this "first played" variable to define the adoption date. In appendix B, I experiment with alternative specifications of "add" dates by using multiple queries per song and reconstructing add dates with more stringent thresholds of how many spins constitutes an add.

Stratified Sample of Songs from 2002 to 2007

Figures 2.6 and 3.2 are based on a stratified random sample of songs released between 2002 and 2007. To sample these songs I first used the year-end format charts for each mainstream format in Mediabase (i.e., excluding Christian and Spanish formats). I then aggregated these charts, summing each song's airplay across formats. For each of these years, I randomly selected a hundred songs receiving more than 5,000 spins and a hundred songs receiving less than 5,000 spins. Since most songs are unpopular, this stratified structure represents an oversample of relatively popular songs. Two of the popular songs and 61 of the unpopular songs could not be queried properly. These missing songs were spread evenly across years. I thus had data on the airplay of 539 unpopular songs and 598 reasonably popular songs, for a total of 1,137 songs.

The Top 25 Songs of 2008 by Airplay

I used the Mediabase year-end "Big Picture" chart for 2008 to draw a list of that year's top 25 songs, as measured by total number of spins in the mainstream formats. I then queried these 25 songs and created a series of diffusion curves for each: the overall pattern, pattern broken out by format, and pattern broken out by corporate owner within format. For the most part I did not use this sample of songs for hypothesis testing but rather to inductively develop a holistic view of how songs diffuse. The only place where I directly refer to analyses of these hit songs is in my analysis of format crossover in section 6.3, where I describe "Love Song" as exhibiting the typical pattern.

New York Attorney General Subpoenaes

In late 2004, the state of New York subpoenaed records from the four major record labels regarding their radio promotion practices. Over the course of the next two years the state settled with the labels and published the terms of the settlements on the attorney general's website, with the subpoenaed documents included as appendices.[1] A research assistant created a database classifying every document in the subpoenas according to what of value changed hands, which stations were mentioned, which songs and artists were mentioned, etc. The subpoenaed documents are available on the New York Attorney General's website, and the author's database summarizing these files is available on request. This dataset was previously used by Rossman et al. (2008) and in this book served as the basis for subsection 3.1.4.

Social Network Survey

The social network data used in chapter 4 was collected by myself and a research assistant through structured interviews with radio programmers. We began by identifying all 181 CHR stations currently in Mediabase as of October 2006. My research assistant and I sent out an e-mail to programmers at the stations directing them to a survey website and followed up by phone. We were able to successfully reach and get usable interviews from 123 stations. The vast majority of the interviews occurred in the fall of 2006, though a few occurred over the course of the next two years. Although my response rate was 68 percent, the nature of social network data means that I observe most but not all arcs, observe out-degree for the stations I interviewed, and have a reasonable measure of in-degree for all stations (whether I interviewed them or not).

The key part of the survey instrument included the questions:

- Which stations do you listen to?
- Which stations do you follow in the trades or monitored airplay data?
- Which stations' programmers do you discuss music with?

Although the instrument distinguishes between types of ties, this was only for reasons of cognitive accessibility, and in analysis I define a directed tie as ego naming alter in response to at least one of the questions. I originally had a wording of "Please name several radio stations who you look to in the course of your programming", but in pre-testing I discovered that the wording was not very cognitively accessible and different programmers interpreted the questions differently. As such, I revised the instrument to ask about three specific ways a station might be aware of a peer's programming decisions.

Programmers sometimes responded to these questions with a description of a set of stations rather than listing specific stations. In a handful of cases such responses were excessively vague, as with a programmer who claimed to listen to "any CHR station in the country." In most cases, though, these descriptions were specific enough to be useful, as with several programmers who claimed to discuss music with corporate sister stations within the same format. Note that the stations' self reports of intra-company conference calls implies that we might see firm-level clustering in airplay behavior, but as seen in chapter 2, this does not in fact occur. My research assistants and I did our best to code such descriptions into specific stations but kept track of which ties were inferred by virtue of meeting the programmer's description rather than specifically named. The results presented in the book include the arcs that were inferred in this fashion, but I also experimented with dropping them. Doing so naturally decreases the network's density but it otherwise has no effect on the overall shape of the degree distribution, the overall structure of the network, or the (lack of) evidence for network contagion.

Unfortunately, the Mediabase panel exhibited appreciable turnover in the three years between querying it to serve as the frame for the survey and querying it for monitored airplay data. This turnover creates a merging problem for analyses that require both social network and airplay data since only the intersection between the 2006 panel and the 2009 panel (or in the case of figure B.2, the 2011 panel) is useful. In figures 4.5 and B.2, the stations that appear in the network data but not the airplay data are shown in gray.

A Note on Anonymity

Most of the data in this book come from sources that are either public record or proprietary but widely circulated within the music industry. As such there is no need to anonymize such data, whether they be analyses of monitored airplay used throughout the book or the New York Attorney General's subpoenaed records used in chapter 3.

In contrast, the network survey data used in chapter 4 were collected under the condition of confidentiality. Thus, I do not label the nodes in figure 4.2 nor say which peers a particular station nominated, nor even which stations agreed to participate in the survey. However, while I cannot say to which stations the programmers of WHTZ are attentive (or even if anyone at WHTZ agreed to talk to me), it betrays no confidence to say that *many* programmers are attentive to WHTZ, so long as I do not say *which* programmers. Similarly, I am free to say that on a particular date WHTZ played a particular song. That is, conditions of confidentiality prevent detailed descriptions of arcs or of out-degree but allow descriptions of airplay behavior and in-degree.

APPENDIX B

ROBUSTNESS TO ASSUMPTIONS ABOUT VOLUME OF AIRPLAY CONSTITUTING AN "ADD"

General Diffusion and "Umbrella"

Most of this book has been about when a radio station "adds," or begins playing, a song. Of course, buried within this is the assumption of what it means to "begin" to play a song. The assumption built into the monitored airplay databases is that the significant event is the very first time a station plays a song. In this supplementary analysis I have replicated figure 2.2 using different assumptions as to how intensely a station must play a song before it can be considered to have adopted it. To do this I collected the weekly playlists for all stations in the Top 40 format for all of 2007 and 2008. I then extracted data on Rihanna's singles and defined a station as having "added" each of these songs when it first played it at least once, five times, ten times, or twenty times during a week.

Subfigure B.1a treats a single spin as an add. This is the same assumption used throughout the book and so not surprisingly subfigure B.1a is nearly identical to figure 2.2.[1] Subfigures B.1b–d define adds more strictly as a week with at least 5, 10, or 20 spins, respectively. These subgraphs actually reflect the ideal-typical constant hazard function more closely than does subgraph B.1a. That is, the curves for "Umbrella" in subgraphs B.1b–d are smoother than that in subgraph B.1a, which is nearly a step function. Furthermore, the later singles now show far fewer early adds leading up to the add date.

Social Network Diffusion and "My Humps"

The analysis of network contagion in chapter 4 would seem to be a particularly poor fit for the assumptions that even trivial usage constitutes adoption and there is no abandonment over the short-run. Fortunately, as shown in figure B.2,

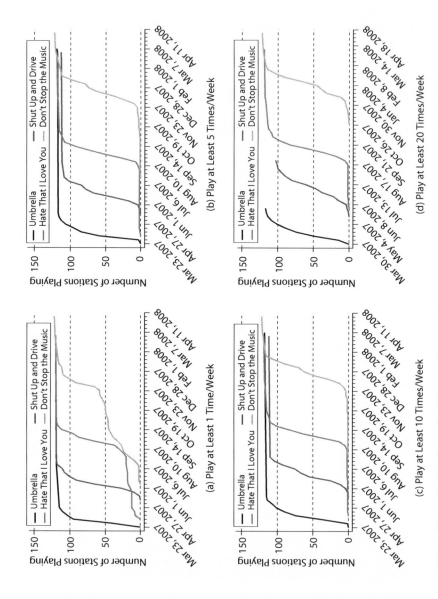

FIGURE B.1. Diffusion Curves for Singles on the Rihanna Album *Good Girl Gone Bad* on Top 40 Stations with Varying Definitions of an "Add"

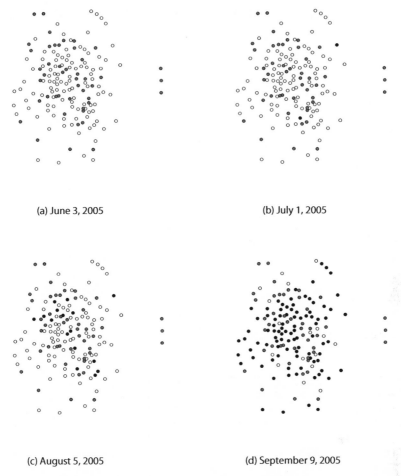

(a) June 3, 2005

(b) July 1, 2005

(c) August 5, 2005

(d) September 9, 2005

FIGURE B.2. Top 40 Stations in Social Network Space with Filled Dots for Those Playing "My Humps" at Least 5 Times in the Stated Week
Note: Gray stations appear in social network data but not airplay data

the analysis proves robust to relaxing these assumptions. In this graph I replicate figure 4.5, but with stations only filled in if they play "My Humps" at least five times in the current week. That is, I require both a reasonably intense use of the behavior to define adoption and I allow stations to exit if they fall below this threshold (or stop playing the song entirely).[2] As can be seen, even with this new set of assumptions the adoption of "My Humps" appears randomly through network space rather than starting in one corner and spreading out like an inkblot, as we would expect if network contagion were the dominant mechanism.

Table B.1
Discrete Time Event History Analysis of "My Humps".

Variables	1	2	3
Number of CHR Stations Named as Alters	0.068	0.001	0.090
	(0.079)	(0.109)	(0.096)
CHR Stations Playing "My Humps"	0.152***	0.143***	0.160***
(lagged)	(0.022)	(0.024)	(0.034)
Number of Alter CHR Stations Playing		0.299	
"My Humps" (lagged)		(0.176)	
Total Spins by Alter CHR Stations of			−0.005
"My Humps" (lagged)			(0.004)
Constant	−10.497***	−10.420***	−10.734***
	(1.935)	(1.932)	(2.265)
Log-Likelihood	−227.318	−226.338	−227.067
$\rho_{station}$	0.925	0.931	0.923
BIC	472.163	474.586	476.043

$n_{spells} = 1058$, $n_{stations} = 80$
Note: Social network ties are directed and so alters are those peers named by ego

Furthermore, some analyses of contagion have found that intensity of alter behavior and not just its presence or absence is important to determining whether ego will adopt (Iyengar et al., 2011). For this reason, in table B.1 I perform a series of related discrete time logit analyses of when a CHR station first played "My Humps." In all models, generalized diffusion through the field is measured by the number of other CHR stations playing the song in the previous week. Contagion through the network is measured by two separate specifications. Model two counts the number of network alters (i.e., stations that the focal station claims to observe) who played the song in the previous week. Model three counts the total number of spins across network alters in the previous week. All models control for out-degree (the number of stations the focal station claims to observe). All CHR stations are used for constructing the independent variables, but only stations who replied to the survey (i.e., those whose out-going social network arcs are observed) are included in the risk set.

The total number of CHR stations playing "My Humps" is a strong predictor of a holdout station's hazard for playing the song. In all of the models, a station that has not yet played the song has less than a 1 percent chance of playing the song if ten other CHR stations are playing the song (that is, a low level of saturation). In contrast, a holdout station has about a 25 percent chance of playing the song if 65 other CHR stations are playing the song (that is, midway to saturation). In contrast, neither of the network variables is statistically significant, and a comparison of the BIC (Bayesian Inference Criteria) test statistics suggests that the model is most parsimonious if one omits these variables. The coefficient for number of alters playing the song appears large, but in addition to being statistically insignificant, it is only one-eighth the size of the general CHR effect when one takes into account that the latter variable has a much higher mean. Likewise, the effect for the total spins by network alters is basically zero. Thus, this event history model supports the less formal analysis provided by figures 4.5 and B.2 that the diffusion of "My Humps" was a generalized endogenous dynamic through CHR and not channeled through social network ties.

NOTES

Chapter 1. Introduction

1. Zoe Chace, "How much Does It Cost to Make a Hit Song," NPR: Planet Money, June 30, 2011.
2. Usage of non-music programs is correlated with age and ranges from about 5 percent of "average quarter hour" for teenagers to about 30 percent for seniors. Arbitron, 2010.
3. For a review of production of culture, see Peterson and Anand (2004). Note that production of culture is superficially similar to older approaches that saw culture as superstructure built on a base of social structure, but in Marxism and functionalism the relation of culture to structure was typically one of vague homology or underspecified assumptions of material interests translating into ideological output. Attempts to seriously think through the underspecified mechanisms of these older models end up in roughly the same place as production of culture (Hall, 1996).
4. For a general review of diffusion of innovation, see Rogers (2003), and for a review particular to sociology, see Strang and Soule (1998). The seminal studies are hybrid corn (Ryan and Gross, 1943), heavy industry technologies (Mansfield, 1961), tetracycline (Coleman et al., 1966), and consumer appliances (Bass, 1969).
5. We use the infelicitous word "hazard" because much of the math was worked out by demographers and epidemiologists predicting death and engineers predicting machine failures. For the same reason, many other technical terms in diffusion analysis (such as "frailty") are cognate with unpleasant things in plain English.
6. This vignette is a stylized account of Coleman et al. (1966).
7. Mahajan and Peterson, 1985; Valente, 1993.
8. This vignette is a stylized account of Ryan and Gross (1943). Hybrid seed corn offers higher crop yields but does not breed true and so must be

purchased every year. This implies both higher output and higher capital outlays. If the corn successfully comes to harvest, this is well worth it, but if the crop fails then the farmer has even more exposure to debt than had he followed the traditional practice of reserving seed from the prior year's harvest.

9. On threshold or cascade models, see: Leibenstein (1950); Granovetter (1978); Banerjee (1992). Also, note that contagion models are usually equivalent to threshold models but they can have different results with certain social network structures (Valente, 1995). For instance, empirical and simulation work demonstrates that under contagion (but not thresholds), highly homophilous networks can result in distinct diffusion patterns with adoptions clustering by such traits as race and with lower overall rates of adoption (DiMaggio and Garip, 2011).

10. Salganik et al., 2006; Sorensen, 2007.

11. Bass, 1969; Mahajan and Peterson, 1985; Valente, 1993.

12. Ryan and Gross, 1943; Coleman et al., 1966; Bass, 1969; Valente, 1993.

13. Pfeffer and Salancik, 1978; Thompson, 1962, 1967.

14. DiMaggio, 1977.

15. MacDonald, 1988; Rosen, 1981.

Chapter 2. How Songs Spread

1. "Umbrella's" trajectory was nearly identical in "Top 40," "Rhythmic," and "Urban" but it later followed an s-curve when crossing over to "Hot AC" (a more rock-oriented flavor of Top 40). As will be discussed in chapter 6, this is a typical crossover format.

2. Please see appendix B for exploration of robustness to different definitions of how intensely a station must play a song before we can consider the station to have "started playing" it.

3. Rossman et al., 2008.

4. Ibid. Also, as will be explored in chapter 6, it is more accurate to say that unknown artists still exhibit an exogenous diffusion pattern *if* they are working within established genres.

5. A year after the initial release of *Good Girl Gone Bad*, Rihanna released a *Reloaded* deluxe edition of the record that featured another three singles. I omit further discussion of these later singles as they were not available to radio stations until after the initial four singles spread through radio.

6. This pattern of promotional campaigns for one product spilling over to related products is well documented (Hendricks and Sorensen, 2009). Likewise, the qualitative and trade literature on pop music promotion includes numerous examples where a radio station will be pitched on one single but opts to play another from the same album. For instance, a programmer explained, "We play records sometimes that are album cuts that the record label isn't asking us to play, isn't a single" (Ahlkvist and Faulkner, 2002, p. 197). The programmer went on to give an example that a particular Lil' Kim single "sucks," but the programmer and colleagues all loved one of her album cuts and played that instead.

7. Foege, 2008; Klinenberg, 2007.
8. DiCola, 2006b.
9. Ibid. p. 43. HHI is defined as $10000 * \sum(\$_i/\sum\$_i)^2$ where \$ is sales and each firm in the industry is "i." When a single firm has a total monopoly, HHI equals 10,000. When an infinite number of firms each have infinitesimal market share, HHI equals zero. The Department of Justice and Federal Trade Commission use HHI as a guideline for anti-trust policy (U.S. Department of Justice and the Federal Trade Commission, 2010). Industries scoring below 1500 are considered to be competitive and most mergers are allowed; those between 1500 and 2500 are placed under scrutiny; and those exceeding 2500 are considered highly concentrated, with mergers being discouraged and market leaders scrutinized for anti-competitive behavior like price fixing.
10. DiCola and Thomson, 2002, p. 61.
11. DiCola, 2006a.
12. This expectation is apparently held by some academic radio researchers, as evidenced by an anonymous peer reviewer who was skeptical of my proposal to apply diffusion analysis to stations playing songs because it was dubious "whether station programmers at such 'large' stations are sufficiently involved in programming decision making to be useful respondents, given the centralization of programming decision-making in the industry."
13. We can relax this dystopian scenario slightly by imagining that Clear Channel had two programmers who split the company's portfolio between them, for instance they might create one playlist for stations in the west and another for stations in the east. In this situation we would have a step function with two steps.
14. Chapter 4 more fully uses social networks to analyze programming.
15. Greve, 1995. Two caveats apply about generalizing from this finding. First, Greve's study pre-dates deregulation and so the radio chains he studied were much smaller than today's giants. Second, that study's outcome was "format flipping," a core strategy change that we would expect to be made by senior management, whereas deciding to begin playing a particular song is the kind of routine decision more likely to be delegated to middle management.
16. Cleves et al., 2004. Readers familiar with multilevel models can consider shared frailty to be closely analogous to random effects. In this analogy the models I have fit are comparable to random-intercept models with no fixed parameters.
17. The standard interpretations of the test statistics show that the amount of clustering is well within chance. However, the test statistics cannot safely be given their usual interpretation because the large number of independently owned stations and small chains impose a conservative bias to the clustering metric. As such, the permutation analysis immediately following this note is much more charitable to the possibility of clustering.
18. Fernandez et al., 2000; Rossman, 2010b.
19. The distribution for the mean shared frailty ($\bar{\theta}$) based on the hundred batches of random data for each song is mean of .1409 with standard

deviation of .0049. Since the standard deviation of parameter estimates from a permutation or resampling approach can be interpreted as standard error for that parameter, this allows us to construct confidence intervals and formal hypothesis testing. The t-test is $(\hat{\theta}_{observed} - \hat{\theta}_{random})/\sigma_{random}$ or $(.1499345 - .1408766)/.0049406$, which works out to a t statistic of 1.833. Thus, not only is the observed clustering substantively trivial, but the t statistic fails to support the hypothesis that shared frailty exceeds chance.

20. Given this absence of a centralized corporate programming effect, one may fairly ask, what is the point of consolidation? First, keep in mind the scope of the finding. Although the findings of this chapter dispel the idea that corporations engage in top-down direction of when to add a song to the playlist, it remains entirely possible that corporations take an active role in the more strategic decision to position the station in a particular format. There is strong evidence that radio corporations use format templates for their stations, as with the "Kiss" branding Clear Channel applies to many of its CHR stations. There is also statistical evidence of format decisions being made at the corporate level, and while this evidence pre-dates deregulation, there is no particular reason to expect that it would be any less true of today's much larger chains (Greve, 1995). It is nonetheless difficult to see why format development would drive consolidation given that before consolidation this service was accomplished quite adequately by consultants. Although there are many reasons why station staff would not be effective at format development, there is no obvious efficiency to treating the service as a "make" service provided by the corporate home office rather than a "buy" service provided by consultants brought in on an as-needed basis to assist with a format flip. Rather, a better answer for understanding why consolidation occurred despite limited effects on programming is suggested by remembering that although programming is the most salient thing about radio to the listener, the musician, and the sociologist, it is not necessarily the key thing about radio to its owners. Broadcasting is a two-sided market where to a first approximation, programming is a means to an end of drawing audiences who can in turn be sold to advertisers (Napoli, 2003; Rysman, 2009). It is on this back-end side that the effects of conglomeration are more clearly seen. From the perspective of programming it seems like a curious coincidence that Clear Channel is not only the market leader in radio but also in billboards. However, when one realizes that Clear Channel is in the business of selling advertising, especially local advertising, it makes perfect sense. For most of its corporate history Clear Channel delegated almost total creative control over programming to general managers so long as they met financial targets for lowering expenses and raising revenues (Foege, 2008). This changed somewhat with Clear Channel's acquisition of Jacor (which, to paraphrase Horace, had the effect that Jacor took captive her captor). However, even the post-Jacor trend toward greater creative control from San Antonio seems to be more at the level of developing formats (for instance, the "hurban" format discussed in chapter 6) rather than micromanaging routine playlist decisions.

Chapter 3. Buying Your Way onto the Chart

1. Slichter 2004, p. 76.
2. Bikhchandani et al., 1992; Salganik et al., 2006; Salganik and Watts, 2008. Note that models of "snob demand" or "fashion cycles" allow that one might place a premium on obscurity, or at least the absence of popularity with the wrong kind of people (Berger and LeMens, 2009; Leibenstein, 1950; Simmel, 1957). Nonetheless, it is easy to overstate the relevance of these models. First, by definition most people have mainstream taste. Second, snobbery may lead one to eschew mainstream hits, but one will still use a popularity heuristic within one's snobbish community. For instance, if a rock snob eschews Nickelback in favor of the Raveonettes, it is notable that the rock snob has chosen to be a fan of the Raveonettes rather than a less famous art-rock band. In the aggregate, such taste heterogeneity is consistent with a superstar distribution for popularity across taste communities (Rosen, 1981). Finally, snob models differ from simpler cascade models primarily in terms of explaining abandonment, but the two types of models tend to be in agreement about initial diffusion.
3. Since most of these demo CDs are unwanted by their recipients, they often find their way to the secondary market, which of course undercuts revenues to labels and artists from sales of new copies of the CDs. Universal Music Group has tried to have its cake and eat it too by stamping such CDs with language like "Promotion Use Only—Not for Sale" and then suing and otherwise intimidating the secondary market for promotional CDs. In a June 2008 summary judgment in the case *UMG Recordings v. Augusto*, the United States District Court for the Central District of California ruled that the "not for sale" stamp is not binding and the secondary market for promotional CDs is legal under the "first sale" doctrine of copyright law.
4. Dannen, 1990.
5. In this context, the word "independent" means that an indie is not directly employed by the record company but is an independent consultant. Despite a similar name (and sharing the slang term "indies"), independent record promoters should not be confused with independent record labels. Indies can be employed by record companies of any size.
6. Since the 1990s, radio stations in the largest markets have generally refused to obligate themselves to indies by selling their playlists (Slichter, 2004). However, in the late 1970s and early 1980s, indies had tremendous influence over stations in top markets such as Los Angeles to the extent that they could veto airplay of popular bands like Pink Floyd that refused to pay their pound of flesh (Dannen, 1990).
7. Coase, 1979; Sanjek and Sanjek, 1991.
8. Communication scholars call such cross-ownership conflict-of-interest between a cultural distributor and surrogate consumer "capitalized payola" or "synergy bias" (Caves, 2000; Williams, 2002).
9. Coase, 1979; Peterson and Berger, 1975.
10. The entertainment industry prefers to refer to product shots as "sponsored entertainment" and has an annual "Madison and Vine" convention

dedicated to the practice. It is completely legal so long as a disclaimer appears (usually in the form of a line in the closing credits of a film or television program that a "promotional consideration was paid by" the sponsor). Product shots have become increasingly important in recent years both because they are seen as "Tivo-proof" and because they are an important part of financing reality television.

11. Fisher, 2007; Sanjek, 1988.

12. Cowen, 2000; Fisher, 2007.

13. Grace Lichtenstein, "Columbia puts Payola at $250,000," *New York Times*, 6 June 1973.

14. Sanjek and Sanjek, 1991.

15. In the 1960s and 1970s, program directors generally gave disk jockeys guidelines on which songs to play and in how heavy of rotation, but the disk jockey had some autonomy within these parameters (Routt et al., 1978). Today program directors typically give disk jockeys an exact music schedule specified down to the minute (Lynch and Gillispie, 1998).

16. Although the details of Wynshaw's testimony focused on soul music, much of the discourse about the scandal elided this genre distinction.

17. Dannen, 1990.

18. The prosecution effort was generally problematic. Halfway through the investigation, the Justice Department fired Marvin Rudnick, the prosecutor who built the case. The stated reason was that he disclosed sealed grand jury evidence, but a popular theory is that this was a pretext and Justice's real objection was to Rudnick's aggressive pursuit of MCA in his trial of Sal Pisello, a low-level gangster who worked for MCA.

19. Dannen, 1990.

20. Not only would indies bill when stations played a song, but a common practice at the time was the "paper add" in which a station would falsely report to the trade journals that it had started playing a song so that the station's indie could bill for the add. This widespread fraud was one of the reasons the labels supported the creation of the monitored airplay services Broadcast Data Systems and Mediabase. These third party data collection services provide data that are both high quality and impartial. In addition to their many legitimate uses, these data allow *credible* payola transactions. Indeed, several of the documents subpoenaed by the New York Attorney General in 2004 explicitly state that pledged bribes will only be honored if the desired airplay is confirmed by Mediabase or BDS. As with other cases in the entertainment industry, the switch from self-reports to passive monitoring has led not only to more accurate data, but also to changes in business practices as participants gain a new cognitive map of the field (Anand and Peterson, 2000; Napoli, 2003, 2011).

21. Dannen, 1990, pp. 323–24.

22. Dannen, 1990; Slichter, 2004; Vogel, 2011. More precisely, in the post-1986 system successful artists entirely pay for billings by indies on their behalf by forgoing royalties until these expenses are recovered by the label. However, most artists never earn sufficient royalties to fully cover their advances, IRP billings, and other recoupable debt. Since the label never fully recovers its

expenses on behalf of these unsuccessful artists, the "recoupable debt" is bad debt and in effect the IRP billings for these artists are still paid in full or in part by the label. Of course in such a situation the artist is not making any money on record sales either.

23. Isgro quoted in Dannen, 1990, p. 296.

24. Williams and Roberts, 2002; DiCola, 2006b.

25. Klinenberg, 2007; Foege, 2008.

26. Eric Bochlert, "Pay for Play," *Salon*, March 14, 2001.

27. Although there were frequent accusations against Clear Channel that it used its power over radio to promote its interests in concerts and vice versa, an extensive analysis of concert ticket sales found no evidence that Clear Channel effectively leveraged its potentially synergistic market power (Krueger, 2005).

28. Mauss, 1967; Zelizer, 1996.

29. Biggart and Delbridge, 2004; Marx, 1967; Polanyi, 1957, 1968; Weber, 1978.

30. Zelizer, 2011.

31. Jouvenal, 2008.

32. Rossman et al., 2008.

33. See appendix A for more details on how these songs were sampled.

34. Rossman et al., 2008.

35. Exogenous diffusion curves were illustrated in figure 1.1 and explained in the surrounding text.

36. DiMaggio and Powell, 1983; Pfeffer and Salancik, 1978.

37. Slichter, 2004. Also, a National Public Radio story estimated that 12 years after "Closing Time," the Rihanna song "Man Down" cost about a third of a million in radio promotion. Controlling for inflation, this is a bit less than "Closing Time," but "Man Down" was also less popular. Zoe, Chace. "How much Does It Cost to Make a Hit Song?" NPR: Planet Money, June 30, 2011.

38. Fligstein, 1990.

39. Coase, 1979.

40. Programmers who admit to accepting promotional support from labels are nonetheless adamant that they only do so for songs which they liked anyway (Ahlkvist and Faulkner, 2002). Even if we cannot take such self-serving denials at face value, they do suggest that payola mostly affects decisions at the margin.

41. Segrave, 1994.

42. Because sales in culture industries have a strong stochastic component, it is debatable how well gatekeepers (e.g., record labels) can estimate which songs will become hits. The best evidence suggests that quality can be measured but success cannot be predicted because quality is a necessary but not sufficient condition for success in cultural markets (DeVany, 2004; Salganik et al., 2006; Salganik and Watts, 2008). While payola is sometimes justified as signaling Thomas Hazlett, "Pay-for-Play" Can Help Musics, *Financial Times*, August 17, 2005. (in the sense used by Akerlof 1970), this is too clever by half since it requires the untenable assumption that record label staff have asymmetrical information about quality over radio station

staff. In fact, it is likely that record label staff are comparable to radio staff at judging the knowable (i.e., non-stochastic) component of popular appeal and thus the (very limited) information is symmetrical (Caves, 2000). About the most that can be said for a "market for lemons" perspective on payola is that it serves as a pre-screening mechanism that saves radio staff the trouble of sifting through the entire deluge of new releases. Such pre-screening saves the stations effort but does not reveal truly private information, so the stations could arrive at the same ends by hiring a larger programming staff or relying on third party screening services such as tip sheets.

43. Dannen, 1990.

44. Ibid.

45. "No aggregate gain in promotional exposure" is a simplification as there will in fact be slightly more promotion overall when payola is pervasive. This is because, on the margin, payola revenues will both support a larger broadcasting industry and convince some broadcasters to target formats that promote high record sales even if they do not necessarily attract high revenues from spot advertising (Coase, 1979). As shown by Entercom's payola revenue targets, record labels are particularly interested in youth-oriented formats like Top 40 and Rhythmic, less interested in older-skewing formats like Adult Contemporary, and of course are not at all interested in Talk radio. Thus, if payola were effectively suppressed, we might imagine less music (and in particular less music of interest to young people) on the radio, which in turn might imply lower record sales. Nonetheless, the record industry would probably benefit overall from a sustained low payola scenario, even if it meant that a few marginally profitable pop music stations would go out of business or flip to Talk.

46. Coase, 1979; Sanjek and Sanjek, 1991.

Chapter 4. Can Radio Stations Break Singles?

1. In the music industry, "to break" means "to popularize" or "to become popular." When used in the transitive sense, the subject is a radio station or its programmer and the object is either a pop single or a heretofore obscure artist.

2. In the context of chapter 3, it is worth noting that these high-status stations also have reputations for integrity. For instance, Slichter (2004) notes that KROQ does not sell its playlist to independent radio promoters. This appears to be distinct from earlier periods, when particularly influential disk jockeys like Alan Freed and Dick Clark are known or strongly suspected to have taken payola.

3. Slichter, 2004, p. 136.

4. Lynch and Gillispie, 1998, p. 87.

5. Snowden and Leonard, 1997; Spitz and Mullen, 2001.

6. Lazarsfeld et al., 1968.

7. Katz and Lazarsfeld, 1955.

8. Rogers, 2003, p. 283.

9. Iyengar et al., 2011.

10. Travers and Milgram, 1969. Note though that "5.7" was the figure for *completed* Nebraska-Boston chains and thus the true figure should be higher. The length that uncompleted chains reached before being broken follows a binomial distribution with a mean of 2.6. On this basis the authors estimate that the latent length of all chains is about two higher than the length of completed chains. However, most people directly or indirectly familiar with the experiment ignore the censorship issue and so nobody speaks of "eight degrees of separation."

11. Barabási, 2002; Zheng et al., 2006.

12. Gladwell, 2000 "The Coolhunt," *New Yorker*, March 17, 1997.

13. Gladwell would be the first to admit that his methods are exploratory given that he relies on convenience sampling, but the essential idea that some people are exceptionally well-connected is confirmed by more formal methods using more representative data (Barabási, 2002).

14. Dodds et al., 2003.

15. Valente, 1995. Also note that Valente found a consistent correlation of early adoption with in-degree (many others report you as a network contact) but in two out of three contexts there was no correlation for high out-degree (you report many others as contacts).

16. Abrahamson and Rosenkopf, 1997; Granovetter, 1978; Watts and Dodds, 2007. An individual threshold is how popular an innovation must become before a particular actor adopts it. Diffusion will be limited if most people have high thresholds and/or there are discontinuities in the distribution of thresholds (Granovetter, 1978). The concept of a threshold can be combined with the economic notion of "reservation price" and include mixes of sensitivity to network contacts (contagion) and people in general (cascades) (Abrahamson and Rosenkopf, 1997; DiMaggio and Garip, 2011; Young, 2009). If an innovation's intrinsic appeal is very close to an actor's individual threshold then that actor may require only one adopting network contact to adopt, whereas if the gap is large the actor may not adopt until many network contacts have adopted (Centola et al., 2007).

17. Abrahamson and Rosenkopf, 1997; Centola et al., 2005, 2007; Centola and Macy, 2007.

18. These figures do not include the 323 nominations for stations in formats other than Top 40. Most of these other nominees were Hot AC and Rhythmic stations, which are essentially rock and hip-hop flavors of Top 40, respectively.

19. Barabási, 2002; Gladwell, 2000.

20. Csardi and Nepusz, 2006.

21. Note that such an association is a necessary but not sufficient proof for the applicability of the opinion leadership hypothesis to radio. Alternate models that can explain the early adoption of prestigious actors include the "riding the curve" effect in which prominent actors adopt a trend just before it would have crested anyway (Lieberson, 2000).

22. This analysis is limited to especially popular songs to mitigate the problem of right-censorship in calculating how a station's add date compares to

the median add date. Specifically, the analysis is based on 146 randomly sampled songs that met the criteria of being played by at least 120 (out of 149) monitored Top 40 stations between 2002 and 2007. Note that restricting the sample only to innovations that diffuse widely is both logically necessary if we wish to compare actors (rather than innovations) and for better or worse is typical of the diffusion literature (Denrell and Kovács, 2008; Rogers, 2003; Soule, 1999).

23. Rogers, 2003.

24. Hua Hsu, "Notes on 'Humps': A Song So Awful It Hurts the Mind," *State*, December 6, 2005.

25. The diffusion of "My Humps" across the Rhythmic format was similar to and concurrent with its popularity in Top 40. However, its diffusion in Urban (another hip-hop format) did not begin until the end of August and seems to be driven by Universal's belated promotional campaign rather than endogenous growth among programmers. Note that an essentially identical diffusion pattern results if one defines an add as at least five spins in a week and allows stations to lapse into not playing the song.

26. The original "My Humps" video consists of the Peas, a few backup dancers, a fog machine, a gray studio backdrop, and some basic props like a pile of steamer trunks and a stationary car. It appears to have been made for a small fraction of the time and money that went into the elaborate game-show-themed video for "Don't Phunk With My Heart."

27. This analysis focuses on adds, defined as the first spin. As shown in appendix B, the analysis is robust to defining an add as five spins in a week and allowing stations to exit when they lapse back below this level.

28. Ahlkvist, 2001; Ahlkvist and Faulkner, 2002; Anand and Peterson, 2000; Rossman, 2008; Sorensen, 2007.

29. There are a few exceptions to these egalitarian algorithms. For instance, Mediabase weights the Country chart (and only the Country chart) by Arbitron ratings, which in practice are a function of city population.

30. Watts and Dodds, 2007.

31. Van Den Bulte and Lilien, 2001; Iyengar et al., 2011.

32. Salganik et al., 2006; Sorensen, 2007.

33. Healy, 2009; Napoli, 2011; Salganik et al., 2006; Sorensen, 2007.

Chapter 5. The Dixie Chicks Radio Boycott

1. An earlier version of this analysis was published in the journal *Social Forces* (Rossman, 2004). That version uses multiple regression methods and demonstrates that each of the findings holds net of the others.

2. Betty Clarke, "Pop—The Dixie Chicks—Shepherds's Bush Empire London," *The Guardian*, March 12, 2003. Like President George W. Bush, the Dixie Chicks are Texans. The "Texas" remark was universally understood as a statement against the pending Iraq war, which began ten days later on March 20, 2003.

3. Diana Heidgerd, "Some Texas Stations Drop Dixie Chicks Tunes," Associated Press, March 14, 2003.

4. The periodic upticks during the Dixie Chicks' descent are weekends. Airplay for all songs increases on the weekend because many stations have fewer interviews, less morning host chatter, and less other non-music content on weekends than on weekdays.

5. Paul Krugman, 2003. "Channels Of Influence," *New York Times*, March 25, 2003. Ironically, were Krugman correct about the chains' actions and motives, this behavior was counterproductive. Although in the following months the FCC continued pursuing its long anticipated "Diversity Index" deregulatory policy, the Dixie Chick's blacklist was the subject of a Senate Commerce Committee hearing which contributed to a backlash against media concentration in Congress Bill Holland "Radio Under Fire: Chick's Ban Comes Back to Haunt Chain," *Billboard*, July 19, 2003 and U.S. Senate, "U.S. Senate Commitee on Commerce, Science and Transportation: Media Ownership (Radio Consolidation)," 2003, and with the general public (Klinenberg, 2007).

6. Wayne Barrett, 2003. "Pro-War Media Conglomerate Tries to Take Over New York: Bush's Voice of America," *Village Voice*, April 2, 2003 and Stephanie Zucharek, "Bush, Shame, and the Dixie Chicks," *Salon.com*, March 18, 2003. Since an earlier version of this analysis was first published in *Social Forces*, most critics of Clear Channel have backed off of this particular charge. Most of these critics now tactfully avoid the issue, but the critical history of Clear Channel, *Right of the Dial*, candidly exonerates the company of being especially responsible for the Dixie Chicks blacklist, even as the book's very title affirms the broader thesis of politicization for which the incident was widely taken as evidence (Foege, 2008).

7. Bagdikian, 2004, p. 134.

8. Halpin et al., 2007. Conservative talk radio became popular in the decade preceding ownership deregulation, so this claim is an example of that rarest of logical fallacies, *pre hoc ergo proctor hoc* (it came before, therefore it is caused by). In 1987 the FCC repealed the "Fairness Doctrine" rule that broadcasters provide ideologically balanced coverage of politics. The FCC's logic was that the policy had created a "chilling effect" whereby stations avoid controversial issues altogether rather than attempt the tricky balance required by the rule. Immediately thereafter, conservative talk radio began its ascent with the syndication of Rush Limbaugh's radio show. By the time ownership policy was deregulated in 1996 and the large chains began forming, conservative talk was already a thoroughly mature format. Despite the temporal flaw in the argument, it is nonetheless interesting that the Center for American Progress/Free Press report does establish that compared to locally owned, minority-owned, or female-owned stations, chain stations are more likely to play conservative talk radio and equally likely to play progressive talk radio (Halpin et al., 2007).

9. Foege, 2008.

10. Foege, 2008; Klinenberg, 2007.

11. Bagdikian, 2004; Herman and McChesney, 1997; Herman and Chomsky, 1988; McChesney, 1999.

12. Useem, 1982.

13. Bagdikian, 2004; Tifft and Jones, 2000.
14. Only corporations with at least 15 Country stations in the dataset are broken out, with the rest lumped into the category "other." To avoid the confounding effects of format, I have limited the graph to just Country stations, but similar patterns occur in other formats. See the *Social Forces* version of this analysis for more information.
15. It is easy to exaggerate the practical significance of Cumulus's ban. First, Cumulus banned the Dixie Chicks only from its Country stations but had no corporate policy as to its Adult Contemporary, Hot AC, or Top 40 stations. Second, Cumulus made the corporate decision to ban the Chicks from Country on March 17, by which time the band had already lost half of their Country airplay.
16. Hall, 1996, pp. 31–32.
17. Alterman, 2003; Montgomery, 1989; Suman and Rossman, 2000.
18. X. "Hollywood Meets Frankenstein," *The Nation* 174:628–631, June 28, 1952.
19. Navasky, 1980. Similarly, once he was exposed as a Communist, folk singer Pete Seeger was "banned from many mainstream venues either because there were outspoken anti-Communists to oppose him or because venues wished to avoid potential controversy" (Bromberg and Fine, 2001, p. 1144).
20. Rossman, 2010a; Tilly, 1983.
21. Montgomery, 1989; Suman and Rossman, 2000.
22. The search engine google.com shows no references on the world wide web to the incident pre-dating the first Associated Press story. Its Usenet archives contain the early references described here. In personal communication, Countrynation.com's editor confirmed how she discovered the story.
23. Associated Press, "Singer's Remarks Rankle Country Fans," March 13, 2003.
24. Curiously, the margin of victory makes little difference. Stations in states where Bush or Gore won with at least 55 percent were similar to stations in states that they carried by bare majorities.
25. Many radio stations use "callout" research to determine when to stop playing a song (Lynch and Gillispie, 1998). This technique involves an automated telephone survey in which a regular panel of listeners rates short clips of current songs. The key figure is the "burn" rate, or the proportion of listeners who have grown tired of a song. Stations typically drop songs when approximately 20 percent of listeners say they no longer like a song. The programmer I spoke to was relying on internal numbers specific to his market, but the callout figures published in the trade journal *Radio and Records* showed that among Country listeners nationally, the Dixie Chicks' burn rate remained below 10 percent even into late March. This implies that those listeners urging stations to blacklist the Dixie Chicks were a vocal minority.
26. Peterson, 1997.
27. Ibid. p. 199.
28. Denisoff, 1969; DiMaggio et al., 1972; Peterson and DiMaggio, 1975; Roy, 2010.
29. Peterson, 1997, pp. 227–28.

30. Victor Davis Hanson, "I Love Iraq, Bomb Texas," *Commentary*, January 16 2003.
31. Rossman, 2004.

Chapter 6. But Which Chart Do You Climb?

1. Greve, 1995, p. 452.
2. Douglas, 1999, p. 351; Lynch and Gillispie, 1998.
3. Negus, 1992, p. 106.
4. Ahlkvist, 2001, p. 347.
5. Negus, 1992, p. 108.
6. Lopes, 1992.
7. Radio's transition to television was greatly abetted by NBC's regulatory capture of the FCC (Wu, 2010).
8. Bass, 1969.
9. Peterson and Berger, 1975.
10. Douglas, 1999; Fisher, 2007; Sanjek, 1988.
11. Douglas, 1999; Fisher, 2007; Peterson and Berger, 1975.
12. Douglas, 1999, p. 225.
13. Douglas, 1999; Fisher, 2007.
14. Many music scholars treat pop as a sort of a semi-genre or "a category that I am reluctant to define as a genre in the strict sense," but which nonetheless has some important features typical of genres (Holt, 2007, p. 17). Notably, whereas the typical genre has a meaningful life cycle, pop tends to experience gradual change over time characterized by incorporating and co-opting developments from the (other) genres (Lena and Peterson, 2008). On the other hand, one of the defining features of a genre is to be characterized by a set of conventions that are explicitly or implicitly understood by consumers and practitioners, with these conventions making possible collaboration and exchange (Becker, 1982; Holt, 2007). Sixty years ago these conventions might have been things like the great American songbook, whereas today they might consist of electronic production technologies like over-dubbing and auto-tune, but at any given time pop has a sound nearly as distinctive as that of any other music genre. Pop is obviously not a typical genre, but for the purposes of this book it makes sense to treat it as one since the relevant concerns here are more about shared expectations than phylogeny.
15. Hotelling, 1929; Steiner, 1952. The Hotelling theorem is best known for its application to politics. The "median voter theorem" predicts that political parties will tend to converge on centrist platforms (Downs, 1957).
16. Berry and Waldfogel, 2001; Sweeting, 2010.
17. DiCola and Thomson, 2002.
18. Alternative is mostly punk and power pop, whereas Active Rock plays more metal. Bands like Franz Ferdinand and Weezer are mostly played on Alternative stations, whereas bands like Disturbed and Slipknot get most of their airplay on Active Rock. Of course, as implied by *Billboard's* combination of the two categories, there is a lot of overlap and bands

like Linkin Park are popular with both Alternative and Active Rock stations.

19. Sweeting, 2010.
20. Hannan and Carroll, 1992; Haveman, 1993; Hsu and Hannan, 2005; Hsu, 2006b; Kennedy, 2008; Zuckerman, 1999.
21. Becker, 1982; DiMaggio, 1987; Hsu and Hannan, 2005; Lena and Peterson, 2008.
22. DiMaggio, 1987, p. 448.
23. Hsu, 2006a,b.
24. Lieberson, 2000. Note that in some cultures names are not subject to fashion because names are constrained by rigid custom. For instance, Republican Rome had only seventeen boys' names to choose from and a girl took the feminized form of her father's clan (e.g., Julia from Julius, Claudia from Claudius, Portia from Portius, etc.) with sisters being differentiated only by birth order nicknames (e.g., "Julia major" and "Julia minor"). Similarly, until fairly recent times most Catholics would be named for saints and Calvinists for names from the Old Testament. The development of the current custom that naming is at the parents' complete discretion is itself an innovation. Thus we have a doubly nested structure of diffusion with any particular name being nested within a fashionable phonemic or etymological genre of names which in turn is nested within the historically unusual cultural assumption that names are appropriate objects for discretion and fashion in the first place (Lieberson, 2000).
25. Fryer and Levitt, 2004; Lieberson and Mikelson, 1995; Lieberson, 2000. Fryer and Levitt (2004) estimate that about 30 percent of black girls born in majority-black California hospitals and 20 percent of black girls born in majority white California hospitals have unique names. Black boys are about half as likely as black girls to have completely unique names, although some masculine names (e.g., "DeAndre") follow similar phonemic rules to those which govern the invention of girls' names. Rather black boys are more likely to have names overlapping with the non-black stock of names (e.g., "Troy") and distinctly black masculine names are usually borrowed from Arabic (e.g., "Malik") rather than invented. Non-black parents are much less likely to give unique names but similarly tend to be more conservative in naming boys than girls.
26. Rossman, 2010a. Note that these scope conditions are unrealistic in many contexts, but are a reasonable description of radio since record labels go to great lengths to make stations aware of singles.
27. Banerjee, 1992; Granovetter, 1973; Rossman, 2010a.
28. Brandner and Strauss, 1959; Ryan and Gross, 1943
29. Negus, 1992, p. 104.
30. Negus, 1992; Slichter, 2004.
31. The necessity of crossover is why few country songs become enormously popular. Although Country is the single most popular radio format, its genre conventions are (or at least are felt to be) sufficiently distant from those of the other formats that few of its songs cross over to other formats.

This despite the fact that in the late 1950s and early 1960s, country substantially diluted its genre conventions as a response to the popularity of rock music (Holt, 2007; Peterson, 1997). Country artists who seek crossover airplay will sometimes change their sound and image accordingly, as Shania Twain did with her album "Up!" Similarly (as discussed in chapter 5), the Dixie Chicks were very successful in both Country and Adult Contemporary, but this airplay was for two different singles, "Travelin' Soldier" and "Landslide," respectively.

32. More than any other format, Adult Contemporary is characterized by Christmas music in December and this leaves little to any room on the playlist to add new songs. However, it is worth noting that "Love Song" began spreading through Top 40 in early fall and so the delay in Adult Contemporary's adoption of the song cannot be wholly attributed to the holidays.

33. This generalization is based on an analysis of the top 25 songs of 2008. See Appendix A for a more thorough description of these data.

34. E.g., Negus, 1992, p. 104.

35. In particular, new genres should be integrated into radio formats during what Lena and Peterson (2008) call the "industry" phase of a genre.

36. Zuckerman, 1999.

37. Fisher, 2007, p. 215.

38. Ironically, radio consultant Lee Abrams was responsible for both the disco station WKTU-FM in New York and the AOR station WLUP-FM in Chicago that based its identity on anti-disco stunts and rhetoric (Fisher, 2007, pp. 216–17).

39. Note that these curves only include stations that entered the database before the song's first add. This is to avoid the issue of left-censorship (i.e., conflating the onset of observation with the onset of action). All of the diffusion graphs in this book omit stations that are left-censored relative to the song being graphed, but this is a more important issue with reggaetón circa 2004 and 2005 than it is for formats at other times because during this period, Mediabase greatly expanded its coverage of Latin stations and (as discussed below) the "Hurban" format developed.

40. The excluded Mexican Regional format is comparable to Country or Polka. It has minimal overlap with the other Latin music radio formats—Spanish CHR, Tropical, and Hurban—which heavily overlap with one another and which are comparable to the English-language formats Top 40 and Rhythmic. In this presentation, the Latin formats other than Mexican Regional are aggregated for several reasons. First, the dataset has relatively few Latin stations so aggregating is necessary to achieve a useful sample size. Second, during this period there was a high rate of format churn, especially with rock stations flipping to Hurban. Because nominal format data are only available at the quarterly level, capturing this rapid churn requires inductively coding format based on the chart with which the station has the closest fit, and the substantial overlap of these formats prevents inductively coding between them with any reliability.

41. Note that, unlike most graphs in this book, figure 6.3 represents a flow of spins rather than a stock of adds. Therefore, the interpretation is only loosely comparable.

42. Agustin, Gurza, "When the Fad Goes Fizzle: The Reggaetón Craze Saw a Quick Burnout With Fans and Radio," *Los Angeles Times*, April 16, 2006.

43. Mora, 2009. The reason that these actors did not simply opt to treat national-origin groups as categories was that Mexicans were numerous but concentrated in the Southwest, whereas Puerto Ricans lived near East Coast political and commercial elites but had a small population overall. In some ways, the creation of a "Latino" category can be read as an alliance, leveraging the sheer numbers of Mexicans with the favorable geography of Puerto Ricans (Mora, 2009). Furthermore this pan-Latin market both imports to and exports from the Latin American market (Dávila, 2001; Martel, 2010).

44. Dávila, 2001; Mora, 2009.

45. Of course, these 1970s trends toward homogenizing American Spanish-language culture echo 1920s and 1930s trends toward homogenizing American English-language culture, such as the development of national radio networks and sound films that largely used the "radio" English dialect (as modeled on "accent-less" Ohio English).

46. Dávila, 2001.

47. Lopez, 1996, 1999; Portes and Rumbaut, 2006. Half of native-born Latinos speak English exclusively at home, and of the half who speak Spanish at home, 78 percent report speaking English very well, for a total of almost 90 percent of the native-born speaking English fluently (Lopez, 1996, p. 155). Speaking Spanish at home is strongly associated with the presence of a foreign-born household member; it seems that many of those native borns who speak Spanish at home are English-dominant but retain Spanish for talking to abuela. Among native-born Latinos with two immigrant parents, 73 percent prefer speaking English, and among those with one immigrant parent, 93 percent prefer English. Latinos who immigrated as young children (sometimes called the "1.5 generation") are less likely to be monolingual in English, but almost as likely to be fluent in English and 61 percent prefer English (Portes and Rumbaut, 2006). These figures are for Los Angeles county. National figures are less detailed but are generally consistent with the Los Angeles data. Latinos also show relatively high rates of out-marriage (Qian, 1997; Qian and Cobas, 2004).

48. Dávila, 2001, p. 72.

49. Martel, 2010, p. 403. Author's translation.

50. Advertising Age, 2009, p. 23.

51. Leila Cobo, "Radio Flips for Reggaetón," *Billboard* September 10, 2005.

52. Sara Corbett, "The King of Reggaetón," *New York Times Magazine*, February 5, 2006.

53. Leila Cobo, "Radio Flips for Reggaetón," *Billboard* September 10, 2005.

54. It is difficult to say exactly how much larger this group of formats became over the period because Mediabase was in the process of expanding its coverage of Latin stations and BIA/fn does not disaggregate between the

various "Spanish" formats. However, in the inductively coded dataset used for figure 6.3, the number of non-Mexican Regional Latin stations roughly doubled between spring of 2004 and fall of 2005. Similarly, radio trade journals reported many stations flipping in to Latin pop formats (mostly "Hurban") during this period.
55. Rossman, 2010a.

Chapter 7. The Future of the Chart

1. Starr, 2004. In the early 1920s many radio stations promulgated ideological, educational, or religious concerns. In the late 1920s, the federal government discouraged these "propaganda" stations in favor of commercial broadcasters supported by advertising (Starr, 2004; Walker, 2001). This policy was endorsed by the D.C. Circuit Court in the 1932 case *Trinity Methodist Church, South v. Federal Radio Commission* (a.k.a., *KGEF v. FRC*).
2. Starr, 2004, pp. 335, 348; Mayer, 1993.
3. Horkheimer and Adorno, 1972, p. 159.
4. Fisher, 2007; Peterson and Berger, 1975; Peterson and DiMaggio, 1975.
5. Duncan, 2004.
6. This is a decline of percent, not percentage points. The average person rating, or chance that the average person is listening to the radio at a given moment, was 17.6 percent in 1989, 16.4 percent in 1995, and 13.8 percent in 2003. This last figure is a lower level than any point since the data series begins in 1976 (DiCola, 2006b, p. 44, based on data from Duncan, 2004). Although that data series only goes through 2003, the comparable "time spent listening" (TSL) figures from Arbitron's annual *Radio Today* almanac is available from 1998 to 2008 (Arbitron, 1999, 2009). The TSL figures also show a steady decline of about 2 percent per year, which corresponds to 21 and 3/4 hours a week in 1998 to 18 and a half hours in 2007. Figures for 2008 and 2009 show a further drop of three hours a week, but these years are not directly commensurable with older data because during these years the Arbitron ratings service adopted the new Portable People Meter methodology, which revealed that the old diary-based ratings had been inflated by about 15–30 percent (Arbitron, 2010; Napoli, 2011, p. 136).
7. U.S. Census Bureau, 2007.
8. DiCola, 2006a,b; Foege, 2008.
9. Neuman, 1991.
10. Were Congress or the FCC to deregulate spectrum allocation, the market would almost certainly reallocate substantial spectrum currently used for broadcasting to wireless telephony and broadband purposes (Coase, 1959; DeVany, 1998; Hazlett, 1998, 2001).
11. Nielsen "The Nielsen Company Measures the *American Idol* Phenomenon," (press release), 2008.
12. Gary Trust, "'*Glee*' Cast Tops Elvis Presley for Most Hot 100 Hits," *Billboard*, February 16, 2011. Note that a figure like total number of singles appearing on the chart is biased toward the peculiarities of *Glee*'s singles, which have

intense but brief bursts of popularity after every episode. By most other measures *Glee* has only a tiny fraction of the popularity or cultural impact of the Beatles or Elvis.

13. Andrew Hampp, "A Reprise for Jingles on Madison Avenue," *Advertising Age*, September 6, 2010, Taylor, 2011.

14. Although Napster was peer-to-peer in the sense that users sent files directly to one another rather than uploading to and downloading from a central server, it still relied on a server to maintain an index of available files. Some subsequent protocols also decentralize the index, which has the practical effect that there is no central hub to be enjoined by court order, only thousands of individual users who provide a much less inviting target for litigation.

15. Kernfeld, 2011; Lehman-Wilzig and Cohen-Avigdor, 2004.

16. Elberse, 2010. Between 2000 and 2008, total recorded music sales declined from $14.8 billion to $8.5 billion. Although digital music sales over this same period went from nothing at all to $2.6 billion, this wasn't nearly enough to make up for the 60 percent decline in CD sales (U.S. Census Bureau, 2007, table 1103).

17. Anthony Bruno, "Fully Loaded Clip," *Billboard*, October 2009.

18. Neuman, 1991, p. 160.

19. Van Den Bulte and Lilien, 2001; Coleman et al., 1966.

20. It is possible to describe any of these alternate diffusion mechanism in terms of network contagion. For instance, field-level endogenous diffusion could be described as cohesive contagion through a fully connected network. Such reconceptualizations are only useful for certain mathematical purposes that require rendering models commensurable as special cases of one another. In theoretical usage the concept of network contagion is best reserved for the kinds of networks we tend to measure, and these have densities far lower than complete connection.

21. Cleves et al., 2004, p. 121.

22. Further complicating matters is that the diffusion mechanism is not purely a biomedical issue but also determined by social circumstances. For instance, sex clubs like bathhouses and Internet technologies like Craigslist and Grindr enable people to find sex partners so casually that sex reflects little or no social intimacy and thus diffusion of STDs becomes more of a generalized endogenous process. Similarly, the risk of contracting HIV experienced by a hemophiliac in the early 1980s or a Chinese peasant today has less to do with the infected status of anyone they know personally than with the general prevalence of infection in the blood donor pool (Binson et al., 2001; Fries et al., 2011).

23. Boushey, 2010; Nicholson-Crotty, 2009.

24. Labov, 2007.

25. Bakshy et al., 2011; Crane and Sornette, 2008; Leskovec et al., 2009; Wu et al., 2011.

26. Bulte and Stremersch, 2004; Crane and Sornette, 2008; Rossman et al., 2008.

27. Dawkins, 1976.

28. Anand and Watson, 2004; Baumann, 2007; DiMaggio, 1977; English, 2005; Hirsch, 1972; Hsu, 2006b; Peterson and Berger, 1975; Regev, 1994.
29. Marx and Engels, 1978, p. 173.
30. Martel, 2010, p. 105. Author's translation.
31. Berry and Waldfogel, 2001; Greve, 1995, 1996; Hotelling, 1929.
32. Leila Cobo, "Latin Radio Flips Boost Ratings," *Billboard*, November 12, 2005.
33. On the other hand, mid-size companies tend to be more specialized by format. For instance, most Radio One stations program Urban and Urban AC, whereas most Salem stations program Conservative Talk or Christian.
34. The obvious exception is that broadcasters *do* need permission from the FCC, an agency that in theory grants broadcasting licenses and can revoke (or "deny renewal of") licenses for broadcasters who fail to serve the public interest. In practice the FCC (with the encouragement of the National Association of Broadcasters) seldom either grants new broadcasting licenses or denies the renewal of existing ones and so most broadcasters acquire licenses on the secondary market. In this respect, broadcasting licenses are not like driver's licenses, which are granted to most applicants for a nominal fee, are nontransferable, and are frequently revoked for misbehavior. Nor are broadcasting frequencies freehold private property since the FCC restricts their usage significantly. Rather, they are most similar to taxi medallions or officers' commissions in early modern armies.
35. McLeod and DiCola, 2011.
36. Podolny, 2001.
37. Pfeffer and Salancik, 1978; Stigler, 1971; Thompson, 1967; Tullock, 1967.
38. Caves, 2000.
39. Gitlin, 1983; Bielby and Bielby, 1994.
40. Wu, 2010.
41. Reality television, which became popular after the repeal of fin-syn, is mostly made by a new generation of independent production companies like 51 Minds, Magical Elves, and Mark Burnett Productions.
42. Napoli, 2011, pp. 106–7.
43. The 2008 court case *Cartoon Network v. CSC Holdings* (aka *Cablevision*) suggests a possible loophole to apply first sale to streaming media.
44. Lehman-Wilzig and Cohen-Avigdor, 2004.
45. Epstein, 2005.
46. Although the Columbia Pictures library allowed Sony to establish Blu-Ray as the standard for 1080p resolution video discs, the format is still less popular than DVD and overall Blu-Ray was a Pyrrhic victory. During the three-year format war with Toshiba's HD DVD, Sony used the Playstation video game brand to promote Blu-Ray. This decision saddled the Playstation 3 model with parts shortages and a high price point at a critical point in its product life cycle, and Sony ceded much of the video game market to Nintendo and Microsoft.
47. For instance, after the death of Michael Jackson unleashed a wave of nostalgia, Sony rushed the post-production of a concert film, *This Is It*,

which it released in theaters on October 28, 2009, or almost three months to the day after the singer's death. Sony considered making the DVD available in time for Christmas but backed down in the face of theater opposition and released the DVD on January 26, probably at a considerable loss of sales compared to a fourth quarter release.

48. Convergence Consulting, 2010. Cable television provides high revenues through carriage fees, in which roughly half of the customer's bill is split up among the cable channels. In general, Internet distribution, whether it is advertising-supported (Hulu and YouTube), subscription-based (Hulu Plus and Netflix), or single episode purchases (iTunes and Amazon On Demand) provides less revenues per viewer than cable. To the extent that consumers use Internet content to supplement their cable viewing, this is a windfall, but to the extent that it is attractive enough to let consumers cut the cord, this implies a net loss for the television industry. To a first approximation, content viewed on a computer screen supplements a cable subscription, whereas that viewed on a television screen replaces it, which is why the television industry is so ambivalent about Internet-enabled televisions and set-top devices.

49. Brian Steinberg, and Andrew Hampp, "Restrictions, Reality Mean Comcast–NBCU Can't Run Wild—Yet," *Ad Age*, January 18, 2011; Joelle Tessler, "Web Video Future at Heart of Comcast, NBC Review," *Washington Post*, December 12, 2010.

50. Jobs became the plurality shareholder in Disney by selling them the Pixar animation studio in early 2006. Although ABC's original deal to sell programming through the iTunes store preceded the Disney-Pixar merger by a few months, the business press treated the iTunes deal as part of Disney's efforts to woo Pixar (Ronald Grover, "Disney-Pixar: It's a Wrap," *Business Week*, January 24, 2006; Nick Wingfield, Merissa Marr, and Joann S. Lublin, "Another Job for Steve Jobs? The CEO of Apple and Pixar Could Face Conflicts of Interest As a Director of Walt Disney," *Wall Street Journal*, January 23, 2006).

51. Nat Worden, "Apple TV Splits Networks," *Wall Street Journal*, September 24, 2010.

52. Hirsch, 1972.

53. Peterson and Berger, 1975; DiMaggio, 1977.

54. Bielby and Bielby, 1994; Waguespack and Sorenson, 2011.

55. Ahlkvist, 2001; Ahlkvist and Faulkner, 2002.

56. FM radio now contains a text channel which often carries the name of the song and artist being played. However, many radio receivers do not display this information and it is unlikely that the FCC would accept a promotional consideration disclosure made solely through this text channel as sufficient.

57. Crane and Sornette, 2008.

58. Matt Cutler, "How to Make Your Online Video Go Viral," *Ad Age*, March 30, 2009.

59. This feud is most infamous for a DMCA takedown notice Scientology sent Google in 2002 over search results linking to xenu.net, which hosts copies of secret documents that Scientology reserves for high-level "operating

thetan" members. The website's name is a reference to an evil space alien described in these esoterica.

60. Janelle Brown, "Fully Loaded Clip," *Billboard*, July 15, 1998.
61. Gladwell, 2000; Travers and Milgram, 1969.
62. Van Den Bulte and Lilien, 2001; Iyengar et al., 2011.
63. Anand and Peterson, 2000; Napoli, 2003, 2011.
64. Abrahamson and Rosenkopf, 1997; DiMaggio and Garip, 2011. Note that although DiMaggio and Garip (2011) frame their analysis theoretically as being about network externalities rather than the flow of information, for my purposes the theoretical framing is less relevant than their model specification's distinction between generalized influence at the field level versus influence that is local to one's immediate alters.
65. Salganik et al., 2006.
66. Anand and Peterson, 2000.
67. Gitlin, 1983; Napoli, 2003.
68. Espeland and Stevens (1998, pp. 329–30). Also see Sauder and Espeland (2009).
69. Anderson, 2006; Salganik et al., 2006; Sorensen, 2007.
70. Digital technology has also increased the accuracy of traditional best-seller lists with "passive monitoring" techniques like Soundscan, Bookscan, the Local People Meter, and the Portable People Meter. Such improvements tend to upset established hierarchies (and provoke hostile reactions from displaced incumbents) as they reveal that country had been undervalued relative to rock (Anand and Peterson, 2000) or cable undervalued relative to broadcast (Napoli, 2011). Nonetheless, correcting who sits atop a best-seller list is a less radical change than completely reconceptualizing market information to emphasize things other than how many people watched, viewed, or purchased something (Napoli, 2011).
71. Bonacich, 1987.
72. Healy, 2009.
73. Weber and Castillo, 2010.
74. Note that information as presented through technologically mediated social networks is currently more oriented toward browsing than searching. That is, it is easy to peruse whatever it is that one's alters are currently discussing, but hard to query for a particular thing to see what one's alters think of it. This is beginning to change. In 2010, Microsoft partnered with Facebook to allow the Bing.com search engine algorithm to make more salient any information that had been publicly flagged by a user's network alters. Facebook's long-term strategic plans involve making information derived from network alters ubiquitous and highly salient to all aspects of media consumption David Gelles, "Facebook's Grand Plan for the Future," *Financial Times*, December 3, 2010. Google has been experimenting with "social search" since 2009 but was stymied by its lack of access to Facebook's social graph. Solving this data problem was among the main motivations for creating the "Google +" social network site in 2011.
75. Napoli, 2011, pp. 82–83.

76. Jack Neff, "What Happens When Facebook Trumps Your Brand Site?" *Ad Age*, August 23, 2010.
77. Napoli, 2011, p. 64.
78. Elberse and Oberholzer-Gee, 2008; Neuman, 1991.
79. DiMaggio, 1987; Lena and Peterson, 2008.
80. Peterson and Berger, 1975; Turow, 1997.
81. E.g., Li, Ogihara, and Li, 2003.
82. Pachet and Cazaly, 2000.
83. Hsu, 2006b.
84. DiMaggio, 1987.
85. Zuckerman, 1999, 2000.
86. The closest analogy to a penalty for hybrid form in a multidimensional context would be an algorithm that recognizes and excludes certain combinations of ranges of values Malcolm Gladwell, "The Formula," *New Yorker*, October 10, 2006.
87. Bielby and Bielby, 1994.
88. Neuman, 1991.
89. Elberse, 2008; Elberse and Oberholzer-Gee, 2008.
90. Bikhchandani et al., 1992; Salganik et al., 2006.

Appendix A. Datasets

1. http://www.ag.ny.gov/media_center/2005/jul/payola2.pdf
   http://www.ag.ny.gov/media_center/2005/nov/Warner%20Music%20Group%20Corp.pdf
   http://www.ag.ny.gov/media_center/2006/may/UMG%20Exhibits%20of%20Assurance.pdf
   http://www.ag.ny.gov/media_center/2006/jun/EMI-Exhibits.pdf

Appendix B. Assumptions about Volume of Airplay

1. There are several reasons why the figures are not exactly identical. First, they rely on queries made at different times, and the scope of the monitored airplay database continually changes. Second, one set of queries defines a Saturday–Friday week and the other a Sunday–Saturday week.
2. Unfortunately, this requires a new set of Mediabase queries and this exacerbates the missing data problem. Mediabase continually changes its panel of stations, and between the time I conducted the network survey (which used the Mediabase panel as a population frame) and the time I collected the fine-grained data about week-to-week airplay of "My Humps," there was a partial mismatch between the set of stations for which I have network data and the set of stations for which I have airplay data.

BIBLIOGRAPHY

Abrahamson, Eric, and Lori Rosenkopf. 1997. "Social Network Effects on the Extent of Innovation Diffusion: A Computer Simulation." *Organization Science* 8:289–309.

Advertising Age. 2009. *Hispanic Fact Pack*. Detroit, MI: Crain Communications.

Ahlkvist, Jarl A. 2001. "Programming Philosophies and the Rationalization of Music Radio." *Media, Culture, & Society* 23:339–358.

Ahlkvist, Jarl A., and Robert Faulkner. 2002. "'Will This Record Work for Us?': Managing Music Formats in Commercial Radio." *Qualitative Sociology* 25:189–215.

Akerlof, George A. 1970. "The Market for 'Lemons': Quality Uncertainty and the Market Mechanism." *Quarterly Journal of Economics* 84:488–500.

Alterman, Eric. 2003. *What Liberal Media?: The Truth About Bias and the News*. New York: Basic Books.

Anand, N., and Richard A. Peterson. 2000. "When Market Information Constitutes Fields: Sensemaking of Markets in the Commercial Music Industry." *Organization Science* 11:270–284.

Anand, N., and Mary R. Watson. 2004. "Tournament Rituals in the Evolution of Fields: The Case of the Grammy Awards." *Academy of Management Journal* 47:59–80.

Anderson, Chris. 2006. *The Long Tail: Why the Future of Business is Selling Less of More*. New York: Hyperion.

Arbitron. 1999. *Radio Today: How America Listens to Radio, 1998 Edition*. New York: Arbitron, Inc.

———. 2009. *Radio Today: How America Listens to Radio, 2009 Edition*. New York: Arbitron, Inc.

———. 2010. *Radio Today 2010: How America Listens to Radio*. New York: Arbitron, Inc.

Bagdikian, Ben. 2004. *The New Media Monopoly*. Boston: Beacon Press.

Bakshy, Eytan, Jake M. Hofman, Winter A. Mason, and Duncan J. Watts. 2011. "Everyone's an Influencer: Quantifying Influence on Twitter." In *Proceedings of the fourth ACM international conference on Web search and data mining*, pp. 65–74. ACM.

Banerjee, Abhijit V. 1992. "A Simple Model of Herd Behavior." *Quarterly Journal of Economics* 107:797–817.

Barabási, Albert-László. 2002. *Linked: The New Science of Networks*. New York: Basic Books.

Bass, Frank M. 1969. "A New Product Growth for Model Consumer Durables." *Management Science* 15:215–227.

Baumann, Shyon. 2007. *Hollywood Highbrow: From Entertainment to Art*. Princeton, NJ: Princeton University Press.

Becker, Howard Saul. 1982. *Art Worlds*. Berkeley: University of California Press.

Berger, Jonah, and Gael LeMens. 2009. "How Adoption Speed Affects the Abandonment o Cultural Tastes." *Proceedings of the National Academy of Sciences* 106:8146–8150.

Berger, Peter. 1967. *The Sacred Canopy: Elements of a Sociological Theory of Religion*. Garden City, NY: Doubleday.

Berger, Peter, and Thomas Luckmann. 1966. *The Social Construction of Reality: A Treatise in the Sociology of Knowledge*. Garden City, NY: Doubleday.

Berry, Steven T., and Joel Waldfogel. 2001. "Do Mergers Increase Product Variety? Evidence from Radio Broadcasting." *Quarterly Journal of Economics* 116:1009–1025.

Bielby, William T., and Denise Bielby. 1994. "'All Hits Are Flukes': Institutionalized Decision Making and the Rhetoric of Network Prime-Time Program Development." *American Journal of Sociology* 99:1287–1313.

Biggart, Nicole Woolsey, and Rick Delbridge. 2004. "Systems of Exchange." *Academy of Management Review* 29:28–49.

Bikhchandani, Sushil, David Hirshleifer, and Ivo Welch. 1992. "A Theory of Fads, Fashion, Custom, and Cultural Change as Informational Cascades." *Journal of Political Economy* 100:992–1026.

Binson, D., W. J. Woods, L. Pollack, J. Paul, R. Stall, and J. A. Catania. 2001. "Differential HIV Risk in Bathhouses and Public Cruising Areas." *American Journal of Public Health* 91:1482.

Bonacich, Phillip. 1987. "Power and Centrality: A Family of Measures." *American Journal of Sociology* 92:1170–1182.

Boushey, Graeme. 2010. *Policy Diffusion Dynamics in America*. New York: Cambridge University Press.

Brandner, Lowell, and Murray A. Strauss. 1959. "Convergence Versus Profitability in the Diffusion of Hybrid Sorghum." *Rural Sociology* 24:381–383.

Bromberg, Minna, and Gary Alan Fine. 2001. "Resurrecting the Red: Pete Seeger and the Purification of Difficult Reputations." *Social Forces* 80:1135–1155.

Caves, Richard. 2000. *Creative Industries: Contracts Between Art and Commerce*. Cambridge, MA: Harvard University Press.

Centola, Damon, Victor M. Eguiluz, and Michael W. Macy. 2007. "Cascade Dynamics of Complex Propagation." *Physica A* 374:449–456.

Centola, Damon, and Michael Macy. 2007. "Complex Contagions and the Weakness of Long Ties." *American Journal of Sociology* 113:702–734.

Centola, Damon, Robb Willer, and Michael Macy. 2005. "The Emperor's Dilemma: A Computational Model of Self-Enforcing Norms." *American Journal of Sociology* 110:1009–1040.

Cleves, Mario, William W. Gould, and Roberto G. Gutierrez. 2004. *An Introduction to Survival Analysis Using Stata.* College Station, TX: Stata Press, revised edition.

Coase, R. H. 1959. "The Federal Communications Commission." *Journal of Law and Economics* 2:1–40.

———. 1979. "Payola in Radio and Television Broadcasting." *Journal of Law and Economics* 22:269–328.

Coleman, James Samuel, Elihu Katz, and Herbert Menzel. 1966. *Medical Innovation: A Diffusion Study.* Indianapolis: Bobbs-Merrill Co.

Convergence Consulting. 2010. *The Battle for the American Couch Potato: New Challenges and Opportunities in the Content Market.* Toronto: Convergence Consulting Group Limited.

Cowen, Tyler. 2000. *What Price Fame.* Cambridge, MA: Harvard University Press.

Crane, Riley, and Dider Sornette. 2008. "Robust Dynamic Classes Revealed by Measuring the Response Function of a Social System." *Proceedings of the National Academy of Science* 105:15649–15653.

Csardi, Gabor, and Tamas Nepusz. 2006. "The igraph Software Package for Complex Network Research." *InterJournal* Complex Systems:1695.

Dannen, Fredric. 1990. *Hit Men: Power Brokers and Fast Money Inside the Music Business.* New York: Times Books.

Dávila, Arlene. 2001. *Latinos, Inc.: The Marketing and Making of a People.* Berkeley: University of California Press.

Dawkins, Richard. 1976. *The Selfish Gene.* New York: Oxford University Press.

Denisoff, R. Serge. 1969. "Folk Music and the American Left: A Generational-Ideological Comparison." *British Journal of Sociology* 20:427–442.

Denrell, Jerker, and Balázs Kovács. 2008. "Selective Sampling of Empirical Settings in Organizational Studies." *Administrative Science Quarterly* 53:109–144.

DeVany, Arthur S. 1998. "Implementing a Market-Based Spectrum Policy." *Journal of Law and Economics* 41:627–646.

———. 2004. *Hollywood Economics: How Extreme Uncertainty Shapes the Film Industry.* London: Routledge.

DiCola, Peter. 2006a. *The Employment and Wage Effects of Radio Consolidation.* Washington, DC: Future of Music Coalition.

———. 2006b. *False Premises, False Promises: A Quantitative History of Ownership Consolidation in the Radio Industry.* Washington, DC: Future of Music Coalition.

DiCola, Peter, and Kristin Thomson. 2002. *Radio Deregulation: Has It Served Citizens and Musicians.* Washington, DC: Future of Music Coalition.

DiMaggio, Paul J. 1977. "Market Structure, the Creative Process, and Popular Culture: Toward an Organizational Reinterpretation of Mass Culture Theory." *Journal of Popular Culture* 11:433–451.

———. 1987. "Classification in Art." *American Sociological Review* 52:440–455.

DiMaggio, Paul J., and Filiz Garip. 2011. "How Network Externalities can Exacerbate Intergroup Inequality." *American Journal of Sociology* 116:1887–1933.

DiMaggio, Paul J., Richard A. Peterson, and Jack Esco Jr. 1972. "Country Music: Ballad of the Silent Majority." In *The Sounds of Social Change*, edited by R. Serge Denisoff and Richard A. Peterson. Chicago: Rand McNally.

DiMaggio, Paul J., and Walter W. Powell. 1983. "The Iron Cage Revisited: Institutional Isomorphism and Collective Rationality in Organizational Fields." *American Sociological Review* 48:147–160.

Dodds, Peter Sheridan, Roby Muhamad, and Duncan J. Watts. 2003. "An Experimental Study of Search in Global Social Networks." *Science* 301:827–829.

Douglas, Susan J. 1999. *Listening In: Radio and the American Imagination, from Amos 'n' Andy and Edward R. Murrow to Wolfman Jack and Howard Stern*. New York: Time Books.

Downs, Anthony. 1957. *An Economic Theory of Democracy*. New York: Harper.

Duncan, James. 2004. *An American Radio Trilogy, 1975 to 2004*. Tesuque, NM: James H. Duncan Jr.

Elberse, Anita. 2008. "Should You Invest in the Long Tail?" *Harvard Business Review* 86:88–96.

———. 2011. "Bye-Bye Bundles: The Unbundling at Music in Digital Channels." *Journal of Marketing* 74:107–123.

Elberse, Anita, and Felix Oberholzer-Gee. 2008. "Superstars and Underdogs: An Examination of the Long-Tail Phenomenon in Video Sales." Working paper, Harvard Business School.

English, James. 2005. *The Economy of Prestige: Prizes, Awards, and the Circulation of Cultural Value*. Cambridge, MA: Harvard University Press.

Epstein, Edward Jay. 2005. *The Big Picture: The New Logic of Money and Power in Hollywood*. New York: Random House.

Espeland, Wendy Nelson, and Mitchell L. Stevens. 1998. "Commensuration as a Social Process." *Annual Review of Sociology* 24:313–343.

Fernandez, Roberto M., Emilio J. Castilla, and Paul Moore. 2000. "Social Capital at Work: Networks and Employment at a Phone Center." *American Journal of Sociology* 105:1288–1356.

Fisher, Marc. 2007. *Something in the Air: Radio, Rock, and the Revolution that Shaped a Generation*. New York: Random House.

Fligstein, Neil. 1990. *The Transformation of Corporate Control*. Cambridge, MA: Harvard University Press.

Foege, Alec. 2008. *Right of the Dial: The Rise of Clear Channel and the Fall of Commercial Radio*. New York: Faber and Faber.

Fries, J. A., A. T. Y. Ho, A. M. Segre, and P. M. Polgreen. 2011. "Using Craigslist Messages for Syphilis Surveillance." In *International Meeting on Emerging Diseases and Surveillance (IMED)*.

Fryer Jr., Roland G., and Steven D. Levitt. 2004. "The Causes and Consequences of Distinctively Black Names." *Quarterly Journal of Economics* 119:767–805.

Gitlin, Todd. 1983. *Inside Prime Time*. New York: Pantheon Books.

Gladwell, Malcolm. 2000. *The Tipping Point: How Little Things Can Make a Big Difference*. London: Little, Brown.

Granovetter, Mark S. 1973. "The Strength of Weak Ties." *American Journal of Sociology* 78:1360–1380.

———. 1978. "Threshold Models of Collective Behavior." *American Journal of Sociology* 83:1420–1443.

Greve, Henrich R. 1995. "Jumping Ship: The Diffusion of Strategy Abandonment." *Administrative Science Quarterly* 40:444–473.

———. 1996. "Patterns of Competition: The Diffusion of a Market Position in Radio Broadcasting." *Administrative Science Quarterly* 41:29–60.

Hall, Stuart. 1996. "The Problem of Ideology: Marxism Without Guarantees." In *Stuart Hall: Critical Dialogues in Cultural Studies*, edited by David Morley and Kuan-Hsing Chen, pp. 25–46. London: Routledge.

Halpin, John, James Heidbreder, Mark Lloyd, Paul Woodhull, Ben Scott, Josh Silver, and Derek S. Turner. 2007. *The Structural Imbalance of Political Talk Radio*. Washington, DC: Center for American Progress and Free Press.

Hannan, Michael T. and Glenn Carroll. 1992. *Dynamics of Organizational Populations: Density, Legitimation, and Competition*. New York: Oxford University Press.

Haveman, Heather A. 1993. "Follow the Leader: Mimetic Isomorphism and Entry Into New Markets." *Administrative Science Quarterly* 38:593–627.

Hazlett, Thomas W. 1998. "Assigning Property Rights to Radio Spectrum Users: Why Did FCC License Auctions Take 67 Years?" *Journal of Law and Economics* 41:529–575.

———. 2001. "The Wireless Craze, the Unlimited Bandwidth Myth, the Spectrum Auction Faux Pas, and the Punchline to Ronald Coase's 'Big Joke': An Essay on Airwave Allocation Policy." *Harvard Journal of Law & Technology* 14:337–567.

Healy, Kieran. 2009. "The Performativity of Networks." Working paper, Duke University.

Hedström, Peter, and Peter Bearman (eds.). 2009. *The Oxford Handbook of Analytical Sociology*. Oxford: Oxford University Press.

Hendricks, Ken, and Alan Sorensen. 2009. "Information and the Skewness of Music Sales." *Journal of Political Economy* 117:324–369.

Herman, Edward, and Noam Chomsky. 1988. *Manufacturing Consent: The Political Economy of the Mass Media*. New York: Pantheon Books.

Herman, Edward, and Robert McChesney. 1997. *The Global Media: The New Missionaries of Corporate Capitalism*. London: Cassell.

Hirsch, Paul M. 1972. "Processing Fads and Fashions: An Organization-Set Analysis of Cultural Industry Systems." *American Journal of Sociology* 77:639–659.

Holt, Fabian. 2007. *Genre in Popular Music*. Chicago: University of Chicago Press.

Horkheimer, Max, and Theodor Adorno. 1972. *Dialectic of Enlightenment*. New York: Herder and Herder.

Hotelling, Harold. 1929. "Stability in Competition." *Economic Journal* 39: 41–57.

Hsu, Greta. 2006a. "Evaluative Schemas and the Attention of Critics in the U. S. Film Industry." *Industrial and Corporate Change* 15:467–496.

———. 2006b. "Jacks of All Trades and Masters of None: Audiences' Reactions to Spanning Genres in Feature Film Production." *Administrative Science Quarterly* 51:420–450.

Hsu, Greta, and Michael T. Hannan. 2005. "Identities, Genres, and Organizational Forms." *Organization Science* 16:474–490.

Iyengar, Raghuram, Christophe Van Den Bulte, and Thomas W. Valente. 2011. "Opinion Leadership and Social Contagion in New Product Diffusion." *Marketing Science* 30:195–212.

Jouvenal, Justin. 2008. "More Static: Independent Labels and Commercial Airplay 18 Months after the FCC Consent Decree and the 'Rules of Engagement.'" American Association of Independent Music Research Report.

Katz, Elihu, and Paul Lazarsfeld. 1955. *Personal Influence: The Part Played by People in the Flow of Mass Communications*. Glencoe II: Free Press.

Kennedy, Mark Thomas. 2008. "Getting Counted: Markets, Media, and Reality." *American Sociological Review* 73:270–295.

Kernfeld, Barry. 2011. *Pop Song Piracy: Disobedient Music Distribution since 1929*. Chicago: University of Chicago Press.

Klinenberg, Eric. 2007. *Fighting for Air: The Battle to Control America's Media*. New York: Metropolitan Books.

Krueger, Alan B. 2005. "The Economics of Real Superstars: The Market for Rock Concerts in the Material World." *Journal of Labor Economics* 23:1–30.

Labov, William. 2007. "Transmission and Diffusion." *Language* 83:344–387.

Lazarsfeld, Paul, Bernard Berelson, and Hazel Gaudet. 1968. *The People's Choice: How the Voter Makes Up His Mind in a Presidential Campaign*. New York: Columbia University Press, 3rd edition.

Lehman-Wilzig, Sam, and Nava Cohen-Avigdor. 2004. "The Natural Life Cycle of New Media Evolution." *New Media & Society* 6:707–730.

Leibenstein, H. 1950. "Bandwagon, Snob, and Veblen Effects in the Theory of Consumers' Demand." *Quarterly Journal of Economics* 64:183–207.

Lena, Jennifer C., and Richard A. Peterson. 2008. "Classification as Culture: Types and Trajectories of Music Genres." *American Sociological Review* 73:697–718.

Leskovec, J., L. Backstrom, and J. Kleinberg. 2009. "Meme-tracking and the Dynamics of the News Cycle." In *Proceedings of the 15th ACM SIGKDD International Conference on Knowledge Discovery and Data Mining*, pp. 497–506. Citeseer.

Li, Tao, Mitsunori Ogihara, and Qi Li. 2003. "A Comparative Study on Content-Based Music Genre Classification." In *Proceedings of the 26th Annual International ACM SIGIR Conference on Research and Development in Information Retrieval*, SIGIR '03, pp. 282–289, New York. ACM.

Lieberson, Stanley. 2000. *A Matter of Taste: How Names, Fashion, and Culture Change*. New Haven, CT: Yale University Press.

Lieberson, Stanley, and Kelly S. Mikelson. 1995. "Distinctive African American Names: An Experimental, Historical, and Linguistic Analysis of Innovation." *American Sociological Review* 60:928–946.

Lopes, Paul D. 1992. "Innovation and Diversity in the Popular Music Industry, 1969 to 1990." *American Sociological Review* 57:56–71.

Lopez, David E. 1996. "Language: Diversity and Assimilation." In *Ethnic Los Angeles*, edited by Roger Waldinger and Mehdi Bozorgmehr, pp. 139–64. New York: Russell Sage Foundation.

———. 1999. "Social and Linguistic Aspects of Assimilation Today." In *The Handbook of International Migration: The American Experience*, edited by Charles Hirschman, Philip Kasinitz, and Josh DeWind, pp. 212–222. New York: Russell Sage Foundation.

Lynch, Joanna, and Greg Gillispie. 1998. *Process and Practice of Radio Programming*. Lanham, MD: University Press of America.

MacDonald, Glenn M. 1988. "The Economics of Rising Stars." *American Economic Review* 78:155–166.

Mahajan, Vijay, and Robert A. Peterson. 1985. *Models for Innovation Diffusion*. Beverly Hills: Sage Publications.

Mansfield, Edwin. 1961. "Technical Change and the Rate of Imitation." *Econometrica* 29:741–766.

Martel, Frédéric. 2010. *Mainstream: Enquête Sur Cette Culture Qui Plaît à Tout le Monde*. Paris: Flammarion.

Marx, Karl. 1967. *Capital: A Critique of Political Economy*. New York: International Publishers.

Marx, Karl, and Friedrich Engels. 1978. "The German Ideology." In *The Marx-Engels Reader*, edited by Robert C. Tucker. New York: Norton, 2nd edition.

Mauss, Marcel. 1967. "The Gift: Forms and Functions at Exchange in Archaic Societies. New York: Norton.

Mayer, William G. 1993. "Poll Trends: Trends in Media Usage." *Public Opinion Quarterly* 57:593–611.

McChesney, Robert. 1999. *Rich Media, Poor Democracy: Communication Politics in Dubious Times*. Urbana: University of Illinois Press.

McLeod, Kembrew, and Peter DiCola. 2011. *Creative License: The Law and Culture of Digital Sampling*. Durham, NC: Duke University Press Books.

Montgomery, Kathryn. 1989. *Target, Prime Time: Advocacy Groups and the Struggle over Entertainment Television*. New York: Oxford University Press.

Mora, G. Cristina. 2009. *De Muchos, Uno: The Institutionalization of Latino Panethnicity, 1960–1990*. PhD dissertation, Princeton University, Department of Sociology.

Napoli, Philip M. 2003. *Audience Economics: Media Institutions and the Audience Marketplace*. New York: Columbia University Press.

———. 2011. *Audience Evolution: New Technologies and the Transformation of Media Audiences*. New York: Columbia University Press.

Navasky, Victor S. 1980. *Naming Names*. New York: Viking Press.

Negus, Keith. 1992. *Producing Pop: Culture and Conflict in the Popular Music Industry*. London: Edward Arnold.

161

Neuman, Russell W. 1991. *The Future of the Mass Audience*. Cambridge, UK: Cambridge University Press.

Nicholson-Crotty, Sean. 2009. "The Politics of Diffusion: Public Policy in the American States." *Journal of Politics* 71:192–205.

Pachet, François, and Daniel Cazaly. 2000. *A Taxonomy of Musical Genres*, pp. 1238–1245. Number April. Citeseer.

Peterson, Richard. 1997. *Creating Country Music: Fabricating Authenticity*. Chicago: University of Chicago Press.

Peterson, Richard A., and N. Anand. 2004. "The Production of Culture Perspective." *Annual Review of Sociology* 30:311–334.

Peterson, Richard A., and David G. Berger. 1975. "Cycles in Symbol Production: The Case of Popular Music." *American Sociological Review* 40:158–173.

Peterson, Richard A., and Paul J. DiMaggio. 1975. "From Region to Class, the Changing Locus of Country Music: A Test of the Massification Hypothesis." *Social Forces* 53:497–506.

Pfeffer, Jeffrey, and Gerald R. Salancik. 1978. *The External Control of Organizations: A Resource Dependence Perspective*. New York: Harper & Row.

Podolny, Joel M. 2001. "Networks as the Pipes and Prisms of the Market." *American Journal of Sociology* 107:33–60.

Polanyi, Karl. 1957. *The Great Transformation*. Boston: Beacon Press.

———. 1968. *Primitive, Archaic, and Modern Economies: Essays of Karl Polanyi*. Garden City, NY: Anchor Books.

Portes, Alejandro, and Rubén G. Rumbaut. 2006. *Immigrant America: A Portrait*. Berkeley: University of California Press, 3rd edition.

Qian, Zhenchao. 1997. "Breaking the Racial Barriers: Variations in Interracial Marriage Between 1980 and 1990." *Demography* 34:263–276.

Qian, Zhenchao, and José A. Cobas. 2004. "Latinos' Mate Selection: National Origin, Racial, and Nativity Differences." *Social Science Research* 33:225–247.

Regev, Motti. 1994. "Producing Artistic Value." *Sociological Quarterly* 35:85–102.

Rogers, Everett M. 2003. *Diffusion of Innovations*. New York: Free Press, 5th edition.

Rosen, Sherwin. 1981. "The Economics of Superstars." *American Economic Review* 71:845–858.

Rossman, Gabriel. 2004. "Elites, Masses, and Media Blacklists: The Dixie Chicks Controversy." *Social Forces* 83:61–79.

———. 2008. "By the Numbers: Lessons from Radio." In *Engaging Art: The Next Great Transformation of America's Cultural Life*, edited by Steven Tepper and William Ivey. New York: Routledge.

———. 2010a. "The Diffusion of Legitimacy and the Diffusion of the Legitimate." California Center for Population Research, Working Paper.

———. 2010b. "SHUFFLEVAR: Stata Module to Shuffle Variables Relative to the Rest of the Dataset." Statistical Software Components, Boston College Department of Economics.

Rossman, Gabriel, Ming Ming Chiu, and Joeri M. Mol. 2008. "Modeling Diffusion of Multiple Innovations Via Multilevel Diffusion Curves: Payola in Pop Music Radio." *Sociological Methodology* 38:201–230.

Routt, Edd, James B. McGrath, and Fredric A. Weiss. 1978. *The Radio Format Conundrum*. New York: Hastings House.

Roy, William. 2010. *Reds, Whites, and Blues: Social Movements, Folk Music, and Race in the United States*. Princeton, NJ: Princeton University Press.

Ryan, Bryce, and Neal C. Gross. 1943. "The Diffusion of Hybrid Seed Corn in Two Iowa Communities." *Rural Sociology* 8:15–24.

Rysman, Marc. 2009. "The Economics of Two-Sided Markets." *Journal of Economic Perspectives* 23:125–143.

Salganik, Matthew J., Peter Sheridan Dodds, and Duncan J. Watts. 2006. "Experimental Study of Inequality and Unpredictability in an Artificial Cultural Market." *Science* 311:854–856.

Salganik, Matthew J., and Duncan J. Watts. 2008. "Leading the Herd Astray: An Experimental Study of Self-fulfilling Prophecies in an Artificial Cultural Market." *Social Psychology Quarterly* 71:338–355.

Sanjek, Russell. 1988. *American Popular Music and Its Business: The First Four Hundred Years*. New York: Oxford University Press.

Sanjek, Russell, and David Sanjek. 1991. *American Popular Music Business in the 20th Century*. New York: Oxford University Press.

Sauder, Michael, and Wendy Nelson Espeland. 2009. "The Discipline of Rankings: Tight Coupling and Organizational Change." *American Sociological Review* 74:63–82.

Segrave, Kerry. 1994. *Payola in the Music Industry: A History, 1880–1991*. Jefferson, NC: McFarland.

Simmel, Georg. 1957. "Fashion." *American Journal of Sociology* 62:541–558.

Slichter, Jacob. 2004. *So You Wanna Be a Rock & Roll Star: How I Machine-Gunned a Roomful of Record Executives and Other True Tales from a Drummer's Life*. New York: Broadway Books.

Snowden, Don, and Gary Leonard. 1997. *Make the Music Go Bang! The Early L.A. Punk Scene*. New York: St. Martin's Griffin.

Sorensen, Alan T. 2007. "Bestseller Lists and Product Variety." *Journal of Industrial Economics* 55:715–738.

Soule, Sarah A. 1999. "The Diffusion of an Unsuccessful Innovation." *Annals of the American Academy of Political and Social Science* 566:120–131.

Spitz, Marc, and Brendan Mullen. 2001. *We Got the Neutron Bomb: The Untold Story of L.A. Punk*. New York: Three Rivers Press.

Starr, Paul. 2004. *The Creation of the Media: Political Origins of Modern Communications*. New York: Basic Books.

Steiner, Peter O. 1952. "Program Patterns and Preferences, and the Workability of Competition in Radio Broadcasting." *Quarterly Journal of Economics* 66:194–223.

Stigler, George J. 1971. "The Theory of Economic Regulation." *Bell Journal of Economics and Management Science* 2:3–21.

Strang, David, and Sarah A. Soule. 1998. "Diffusion in Organizations and Social Movements: From Hybrid Corn to Poison Pills." *Annual Review of Sociology* 24:265–290.

Suman, Michael, and Gabriel Rossman. 2000. *Advocacy Groups and the Entertainment Industry*. Westport, CT: Praeger.

163

Sweeting, Andrew. 2010. "The Effects of Mergers on Product Positioning: Evidence from the Music Radio Industry." *RAND Journal of Economics* 41:372–397.

Taylor, Timothy D. 2011. *The Sounds of Capitalism: Advertising, Music, and the Conquest of Culture*. Chicago: University of Chicago Press.

Thompson, James. 1967. *Organizations in Action: Social Science Bases of Administrative Theory*. New York: McGraw-Hill.

Thompson, James D. 1962. "Organizations and Output Transactions." *American Journal of Sociology* 68:309–324.

Tifft, Susan E., and Alex S. Jones. 2000. *The Trust*. Boston: Little, Brown, and Company.

Tilly, Charles. 1983. "Speaking Your Mind Without Elections, Surveys, or Social Movements." *Public Opinion Quarterly* 47:461–478.

Travers, Jeffrey, and Stanley Milgram. 1969. "An Experimental Study of the Small World Problem." *Sociometry* 32:425–443.

Tullock, Gordon. 1967. "The Welfare Cost of Tariffs, Monopolies, and Theft." *Economic Inquiry* 5:224–232.

Turow, Joseph. 1997. *Breaking Up America: Advertisers and the New Media World*. Chicago: University of Chicago Press.

U.S. Census Bureau. 2007. *Statistical Abstract of the United States, 2008*. Washington, DC: U.S. Census Bureau, 127th edition.

U.S. Department of Justice and the Federal Trade Commission. 2010. *Horizontal Merger Guidelines*. Washington, DC: U.S. Federal Trade Commission.

Useem, Michael. 1982. "Classwide Rationality in the Politics of Managers and Directors of Large Corporations in the United States and Great Britain." *Administrative Science Quarterly* 27:199–226.

Valente, Thomas W. 1993. "Diffusion of Innovations and Policy Decision-Making." *Journal of Communication* 43:30–45.

———. 1995. *Network Models of the Diffusion of Innovations*. Cresskill, NJ: Hampton Press.

Van Den Bulte, Christophe, and Gary L. Lilien. 2001. "Medical Innovation Revisited: Social Contagion versus Marketing Effort." *American Journal of Sociology* 106:1409–1435.

Van Den Bulte, Christophe, and Stefan Stremersch. 2004. "Social Contagion and Income Heterogeneity in New Product Diffusion: A Meta-Analytic Test." *Marketing Science* 23:530–544.

Vogel, Harold. 2011. *Entertainment Industry Economics: A Guide for Financial Analysis*. Cambridge, UK: Cambridge University Press, 8th edition.

Waguespack, David M., and Olav Sorenson. 2011. "The Ratings Game: Asymmetry in Classification." *Organization Science* 22:541–553.

Walker, Jesse. 2001. *Rebels on the Air: An Alternative History of Radio in America*. New York: New York University Press.

Watts, Duncan J., and Peter Sheridan Dodds. 2007. "Influentials, Networks, and Public Opinion Formation." *Journal of Consumer Research* 34:441–458.

Weber, Ingmar, and Carlos Castillo. 2010. "The Demographics of Web Search." In *Proceedings of the 33rd International ACM SIGIR Conference on Research and Development in Information Retrieval*, pp. 523–530, Geneva, Switzerland. ACM.

Weber, Max. 1978. *Economy and Society: An Outline of Interpretive Sociology.* Berkeley: University of California Press.

Williams, Dmitri. 2002. "Synergy Bias: Conglomerates and Promotion in the News." *Journal of Broadcasting & Electronic Media* 46:453–472.

Williams, George, and Scott Roberts. 2002. "Radio Industry Review 2002: Trends in Ownership, Format, and Finance." Federal Communications Commission Research Paper.

Wu, Shaomei, Jake M. Hofman, Winter A. Mason, and Duncan J. Watts. 2011. "Who Says What to Whom on Twitter." In *Proceedings of the 20th International Conference on World Wide Web*, pp. 705–714. ACM.

Wu, Tim. 2010. *The Master Switch: The Rise and Fall of Information Empires.* New York: Alfred A. Knopf.

X. 1952. "Hollywood Meets Frankenstein." *Nation* 174:628–631.

Young, H. Peyton. 2009. "Innovation Diffusion in Heterogeneous Populations: Contagion, Social Influence, and Social Learning." *American Economic Review* 99:1899–1924.

Zelizer, Viviana A. 1996. "Payments and Social Ties." *Sociological Forum* 11:481–495.

———. 2011. *Economic Lives: How Culture Shapes the Economy.* Princeton, NJ: Princeton University Press.

Zheng, Tian, Matthew J. Salganik, and Andrew Gelman. 2006. "How Many People Do You Know in Prison?: Using Overdispersion in Count Data to Estimate Social Structure in Networks." *Journal of the American Statistical Association* 101:409–423.

Zuckerman, Ezra W. 1999. "The Categorical Imperative: Securities Analysts and the Illegitimacy Discount." *American Journal of Sociology* 104:1398–1438.

———. 2000. "Focusing the Corporate Product: Securities Analysts and De-Diversification." *Administrative Science Quarterly* 45:591–619.

INDEX

Page numbers followed by *f* indicate figures.

future of the chart: advertising and
(*continued*)
and, 94, 99–100, 103, 108–13, 120;
regulation and, 99, 102, 105, 107, 110;
salient information structures and,
112–16; social networks and, 95–96,
99–100, 104, 112, 115–16, 120;
streaming media and, 92, 94, 104–7,
111, 116–18; Top 40 stations and, 99
Future of the Mass Audience (Neuman), 108

Gambino family, 28–30
Garofalo, Janeane, 65
gatekeeping, 120, 139n42; accumulation
of fame and, 8; algorithmic, 112;
best-seller lists and, 113; controlling
publicity and, 108; genre and, 119;
Hirsch model of, 7, 23; pop music
and, 99; salient information structures
and, 112–13, 116
Gay and Lesbian Alliance Against
Defamation, 64
GE, 91
Genius algorithm, 115
genre 24, 115–120; art and, 75–77;
classification and, 75–77; clusters and,
76; folk, 67, 80, 144n19; hip-hop, 10,
53, 72, 78–89, 102–3, 117–18, 141n18,
142n25 (*see also* Rhythmic, Urban);
ideological connotations of 67–69; old
timey, 67; reggaetón, 9, 72, 81–90,
100, 102, 116, 147n39 (*see also*
Hurban); new wave, 45, 118; punk, 45,
59, 69, 80–81, 118, 145n18 (*see also*
Active Rock, Alternative); R&B, 25;
rock, 7, 25–28, 34, 44–45, 59, 69,
72–81, 118, 134n1, 137n2, 146n31,
153n70; soul, 27, 74, 138n16. *See also*
format
German Ideology, The (Marx), 100–101
"Get Retarded" (Black Eyed Peas), 53
gifts, 24, 30–34, 39, 109
Giuliani, Rudy, 28, 38, 42
Gladwell, Malcolm, 47–48
Glee (TV show), 93, 107
Good Girl Gone Bad (Rihanna), 13–15, 54,
128*f*, 134n5
Goodman, Howard, 29
Google, 144n22; bombing and, 111;
Books, 105; PageRank and, 58, 95,
111, 114; Google +, 153n74; Google

TV, 106; Scientology and, 152n59;
search engine optimization and, 111
Gotti, John, 28
Gould, William W., 96
Grand Upright v. Warner, 103
Guardian, The (newspaper), 59, 62, 64–65,
69, 142n2
Guiding Light (TV show), 73
Guns N' Roses, 74
Gutierrez, Roberto G., 96

Harris hearings, 26, 38
"Hate That I Love You" (Rihanna), 13–15,
128*f*
"Have You Forgotten" (Worley), 68
hazard: baseline, 96–97; constant, 4, 21,
77–79, 89, 96, 127; corporate radio
and, 21; Cox proportional hazards
model and, 96; crossover and, 77–79;
endogenous, 5, 47; exogenous, 15;
exponential growth and, 4–5; holdouts
and, 14, 130; "My Humps" and, 55;
opinion leaders and, 47; over time, 4,
96; prior adoptions and, 5; record
release dates and, 14–15; risk pool
and, 3–5; role of influentials and, 55;
use of term, 133n5
HDTV, 106
Hedström, Peter, 97
Hendrix, Jimi, 28
Herfindahl-Hirschman Index, 15, 135n9
Herman, Edward, 64
"Hey Mama" (Black Eyed Peas), 53
High Noon (film), 68
High School Musical (record album), 92–93
hillbillies, 65, 67
hip-hop, 10; breaking singles and, 53,
141n18, 142n25; centralization and,
102–3; crossover and, 78–79; format
trends and, 72; genre and, 117–18;
Mexican Americans and, 88; reggaetón
and, 81–89
Hirsch, Paul, 6–7, 108
HIV, 47, 96–97, 144n22, 150n22
holdouts, 130; early adopters and, 15,
46–48, 82, 85–86, 96, 141nn15,21;
innovation and, 5, 14; property rights
and, 103, 105; transaction costs and,
102
Home (Dixie Chicks), 59
Horkheimer, Max, 91

Horowitz, David, 41

Hot 100 chart, 71, 74, 93, 149n12

Hot AC, 68, 77–79, 134n1, 141n18, 144n15

House Committee on Un-American Activities (HUAC), 64

Hubbard, L. Ron, 111

Hulu, 106–7, 152n48

Hurban, 9, 72, 136n20, 147n39; advertising and, 83, 85–88; airplay for, 83–85; centralization and, 102; Clear Channel Communications and, 88, 102; crossover and, 84, 89; genre and, 116; growing Latino population and, 85; KXOL and, 85; market niche of, 83–90; Mexican Regional and, 83–85, 88–89, 147n40, 148n54; reggaetón and, 83–90; Spanish language and, 85–86, 148n47

iCloud, 1

ideal types, 3, 46

ideologies: artistic creativity and, 32; centralization and, 100–101; Country and, 67–70; cowboys and, 67–68; distortions of, 63; Fairness Doctrine and, 143n8; future of the chart and, 149n1; Marxism and, 61, 63, 70, 133n3; Texas and, 67–68

indies (independent radio promoters (IRPs)), 24, 109; boycotts of, 28–31, 41–42; Clear Channel Communications and, 36; meaning of term, 137n5; paper adding and, 138; payola and, 24, 28–34, 38–42, 138nn20,22; phoner compaigns and, 34–35; selling playlists and, 137n6, 140n2

influentials: contagion and, 56–58; endogenous diffusion and, 53–58; peer influence and, 53–58; promotion and, 54–58; social networks and, 57–58

innovation, 133n4, 141n22; adoption mechanisms and, 95–100; baseline hazard and, 96–97; business models and, 35, 38–39, 42–43, 72, 94, 106–7; competition and, 98; computing power and, 95, 97–98; contagion and, 95–97; corporate radio and, 19; Cox proportional hazards model and, 96; custom and, 146n24; diffusion of, 2–6

(see also diffusion); disruptive, 107; early adopters and, 15, 46–48, 82, 85–86, 96, 141nn15,21; established business model and, 94; external influences and, 4–5, 95, 97, 111, 123; fin-syn rule and, 103–4; formats and, 73, 76, 90, 94; future of the chart and, 94–99, 104, 107; general lessons for, 95–100; holdouts and, 5, 14; impacts of, 2–3; Moore's Law and, 95; opinion leaders and, 46–48; popularity and, 141n16; risk pool and, 3–5; salient information structures and, 112–16; search engine optimization and, 111; semiparametric survival models and, 96; sorts of, 35–36, 95–98; vertical integration and, 64, 103–7

instruments, 22, 67, 77, 80–81

intellectual property rights: *Bridgeport v. Dimension* and, 103; copyright and, 104, 137n3; decision-making and, 103–8; Digital Rights Management and, 106; first sale doctrine and, 104, 137n3, 151n43; format and, 102–3; Google Books and, 105; *Grand Upright v. Warner* and, 103; holdout rights and, 103, 105; imitation and, 102–3; Napster and, 93, 150n14; payola and, 24, 26, 37, 109; peer-to-peer file sharing and, 93, 104, 106, 150n14; piracy and, 94; publicity and, 109; sampling and, 103, 135n19, 141n13; streaming media and, 1, 105 (see also streaming media); UCLA and, 105; Video Furnace and, 105

internal influences, 5, 111. *See also* contagion, diffusion, peer influence, and s-curves

Internet Relay Chat (IRC), 93

iPad, 107

iPod, 33, 53, 93

Irish Americans, 76, 88

Irish folk, 80–81

Isgro, Joe, 28–29, 39, 43

Island (record label), 72

iTunes, 22, 93, 104, 106, 115, 118, 152nn48,50

Ivy Queen, 81

Jacks, Kelso, 45

Jackson, Michael, 151n47

video player standards, 105–6
vinyl, 94
viral marketing, 11, 47–49, 98, 111
Virgin, 34
vocal coaches, 1, 93
voice tracking, 16
voters, 45–46, 145n15

wall of women, 71
Wall Street Journal, 107
WalMart, 22
Warner, 28, 31, 34, 41–42, 103, 106
WARQ, 34
washing machines, 2
Watts, Duncan J., 112
WBLI, 33
WEAF, 91
Weatherly, Kevin, 45
Weavers, The (musical group), 67
Westinghouse, 91
WFLZ, 50
Who, The, 42
WHTZ, 49–51, 55–57, 126
Wild Orchid (band), 53
Wisin y Yandel, 81
WKDF, 65
WKFS, 55–56

WKSE, 31, 33
WKTU, 147n38
WLUP, 80
WNCI, 50
word-of-mouth diffusion, 4–5, 95, 99, 115
Wordpress, 115
Worley, Darryl, 68
WSJ.com, 107
WSTW, 33
Wu, Shaomei, 105
WVOZ, 88
Wynshaw, David, 27, 41, 138n16
WZNE, 32–33
WZYP, 57

X (punk band), 45

YouTube: cultural diffusion on, 98; disclosure and, 110–11; external influence and, 111; future of the chart and, 94, 98, 106, 110–12, 152n48; internal influence and, 111; music videos and, 94; sponsors and, 110–11

Zeno's paradox, 4–5. *See also* concave curves